THE CIVILIAN CONSERVATION — CORPS — COOKBOOK

THE CIVILIAN CONSERVATION — CORPS — COOKBOOK

AMY BIZZARRI

AMERICAN PALATE

Published by American Palate
A Division of The History Press
Charleston, SC
www.historypress.com

First published 2023

Manufactured in the United States

ISBN 9781467153263

Library of Congress Control Number applied for.

Grant, dear Lord, that our hearts may be filled with the love of nature, and teach us to commune with her invisible forms.

Give us, we pray Thee, ears to hear her voice of gladness; eyes to see her smile of beauty, and souls to feel her messages of love.

As the balsam of the pine tree heals our infirmities, so also may the balsam of Thy love heal the heart that is heavy and sad.

As the cedars of Lebanon and the trees of Olivet bear silent witness to the physical presence of the Great Teacher, so may the work of the CCC bear evidence of the work of our hands and the spirit of our willingness to serve.

Help us, dear Lord, to realize that true happiness lies not in what we give but in what we share.

May we therefore serve as living examples of cheerfulness, thankfulness, loyalty, and devotion.

And finally, when our enrollment period is over; when recall has been sounded and our last good deed has been done, may the Supreme Forester of the universe invite us to eat of the tree of life, which is in the midst of the paradise of God.

—C.L. McMahan, educational advisor,
CCC Company 506, Pedro, Ohio

Dedicated to the memory of my grandfather Russell Lofthouse; CCC Company 797; CCC Camps BF1 in Foxholm, North Dakota; and CCC Camp BF-3, Kenmare, North Dakota, August 1935–April 1937

A Civilian Conservation Corps enrollee plants a tree in Montana. Working at a labor-intensive CCC camp meant enrollees burned more than four thousand calories a day. This made food important from a crew health standpoint; after all, if workers were not feeling well, they would be unable to perform their assigned duties. *Fotosearch/Getty Images.*

Special thanks to Nicky Ball, interpretive naturalist, Pokagon State Park and Trine SRA; Dave Stack, the National Museum of Forest Service History, forestservicemuseum.org; Phil Naud.

CONTENTS

Across the country, most CCC camps were segregated. In Oregon, however, Black and white men worked and lived together. There were reportedly no problems. But when southern lawmakers heard about the mixed-race camps, they demanded they be segregated. *National Forest Service*.

PREFACE

In these days of difficulty, we Americans everywhere must and shall choose the path of social justice…the path of faith, the path of hope, and the path of love toward our fellow man.
—Franklin Delano Roosevelt, October 2, 1932

South Dakota, 1935. My grandfather Russell Lofthouse was one of the millions of young, unemployed Americans. He was born in Chicago on August 17, 1915. His father had died a few years prior of alcoholism, and his mother was dying of tuberculosis in the Chicago Municipal Tuberculosis Sanitarium. After losing his job as a shipping clerk at the Stewart Printing Company in Chicago, my grandfather moved to Powers Lake, South Dakota, to secure work as a laborer on a farm owned by his uncle Julius Anderson. When he enrolled in CCC Camp 797 / BF-3 on August 31, 1935, he stood 5 feet, 11 inches and weighed a mere 153 pounds.

On his enrollment papers, he was noted to have one year of high school under his belt. He had been a Boy Scout. His vision was 20-20. His character was judged as "excellent."

More than fifteen million Americans were unemployed in 1930. Though President Herbert Hoover urged "patience and self-reliance," as the United States endured what he called a mere "passing incident in our national lives," suffering was widespread. Though the root causes of recession had been simmering for years—increasing wealth disparity and purchasing power, the worldwide instability after World War I—the stock market crash of October 29, 1929, launched the challenging era known as the Great Depression.

With no government-provided insurance or compensation for the unemployed, spending and then the consumer economy came to a standstill. More than nine thousand United States–based banks closed between 1930 and 1933, wiping out more than $2.5 billion in deposits. As President Hoover believed that solving such problems was not the job of the federal government, Hoovervilles (homeless encampments) popped up across the country as more and more people lost their homes to the crisis. Natural disasters added to the struggle: dust storms and droughts carried away soil, making it next to impossible to plant crops as the Dust Bowl headed from the Plains states west to California. Deaths from suicide increased by a whopping 22.8 percent between 1929 and 1932.

But in 1932, Americans put all their hopes in a new president when Franklin Delano Roosevelt defeated Republican incumbent Herbert Hoover in one of the largest landslide victories in U.S. history. Roosevelt

President Franklin D. Roosevelt made his first visit to a CCC camp, Camp Fechner, at Big Meadows in Shenandoah National Park, Virginia, in the early summer of 1933. Seated at the table are, *from left to right*: Major General Paul B. Malone, commanding general of the Third Corps Area; Louis Howe, secretary to the president; Secretary of the Interior Harold L. Ickes; Robert Fechner, director of the CCC; the president; Secretary of Agriculture Henry A. Wallace; and Assistant Secretary of Agriculture Rexford G. Tugwell. *NPS*.

An impoverished American family living in a shanty in Elm Grove, Oklahoma County, Oklahoma, 1936, photographed by Dorothea Lange. Lange was a photojournalist, best known for her Depression-era work for the Farm Security Administration. *Library of Congress.*

Left: "I propose to create a Civilian Conservation Corps to be used in simple work....More important, however, than the material gains will be the moral and spiritual value of such work." Franklin Delano Roosevelt, March 21, 1933. *National Archives via Wikimedia Commons.*

Right: President Theodore Roosevelt (*left*) and nature preservationist John Muir, founder of the Sierra Club, on Glacier Point in Yosemite National Park. In the background are upper and lower Yosemite Falls. Franklin Delano Roosevelt's focus on the conservation and restoration of the American landscape mirrors that of his cousin Theodore Roosevelt, who, after becoming president in 1901, closed over 230 million acres to commercial development, establishing 150 national forests, 51 federal bird reserves, 4 national game preserves, 5 national parks and 18 national monuments. *Underwood and Underwood; Library of Congress.*

pledged to use the power of the federal government to make life better for all Americans. "I pledge myself," he said, "to a New Deal for the American people." Later, he noted, "The test of our progress is not whether we add more to the abundance of those who have much; it is whether we provide enough for those who have too little."

During his first one hundred days in office, FDR waged "a war against the emergency." "The only thing we have to fear is fear itself," he reminded Americans in his inaugural address. By June, FDR and Congress had passed fifteen major laws, including the Agricultural Adjustment Act, the Home Owners' Loan Act and the National Industrial Recovery Act.

On March 21, 1933, FDR proposed another project to tackle mass unemployment. "I propose to create a Civilian Conservation Corps to be used in simple work," he said. "More important, however, than the material gains will be the moral and spiritual value of such work."

Robert Fechner, the first director of the CCC, wrote, "The major objectives of this new venture in social relief were to give jobs to hundreds of thousands of discouraged and undernourished young men, idle through no fault of their own, to build up these young men physically and spiritually, and to start the nation on a sound conservation program which would conserve and expand our timber resources, increase recreational opportunities and reduce the annual toll take by the forest fire, disease, pests, soil erosion and floods." *Harris & Ewing, photographer; Library of Congress.*

Frances Perkins served as the United States secretary of labor from 1933 to 1945, the longest serving in that position and the first woman ever to serve in a presidential cabinet. "She was a moving force. Without her, Social Security doesn't exist, and without her, the nationwide unemployment insurance program doesn't exist," said Kirstin Downey, who spent a decade studying Perkins's life and documented it in the book *The Woman Behind the New Deal. Library of Congress.*

The major objectives of this new venture in social relief were to give jobs to hundreds of thousands of discouraged and undernourished young men, idle through no fault of their own, to build up these young men physically and spiritually, and to start the nation on a sound conservation program which would conserve and expand our timber resources, increase recreational opportunities and reduce the annual toll take by the forest fire, disease, pests, soil erosion, and floods.

—Robert Fechner, the first director of the Civilian Conservation Corps (1933–39), April 22, 1936

Originally known as the Emergency Conservation Work program, the CCC offered young, single men between the ages of eighteen and twenty-five meals, lodging and, most importantly, the opportunity to enlist in work programs that not only paid $30 a month ($25 of which would be sent straight to their families back home) but also offered the chance to receive valuable vocational training or complete their high school education.

FDR chose Robert Fechner, the vice president of the American Federation of Labor, to be the national director of the CCC. Frances Perkins, the first female cabinet officer in U.S. history, was tasked with coordinating the recruitment and selection of CCC enrollees. The army would provide the clothing and manage the camps; work projects were organized by the U.S. Forest Service, U.S. Park Service, Soil Conservation Service, U.S. Fish and Wildlife Service, Bureau of Land Management and the Bureau of Reclamation.

The typical CCC enrollee was an unemployed, unmarried male. He came from a family of six, and his father was likely unemployed. Upon passing a physical exam, enrollees served a minimum six-month period, with the option to serve for up to two years. The enrollees worked forty hours per week, five days a week.

While the main goal of the CCC was to provide financial support and boost morale at a time when unemployment had reached 25 percent,

A typical Civilian Conservation Corps enrollee, hard at work with a smile. Angeles National Forest, California, March 1939. *National Forest Service, photo by F.E. Dunham.*

America's public lands, forests and parks would also benefit: CCC projects were focused on restoring and protecting our nation's natural resources. The CCC planted trees, fought forest fires and stocked streams with fish. They built bridges, fire lookout towers, campgrounds, picnic grounds and service buildings at state and national parks, many of which are still enjoyed today.

When they weren't on the work site, the enrollees furthered their educations. They received valuable job training and learned countless skills. They enjoyed recreational sports—football, baseball and basketball were the most popular—pool, ping-pong. Each camp featured a library with two hundred–plus books on the shelves. Most camps produced their own newsletters, and the national CCC newsletter, the aptly titled *Happy Days*, was a popular read.

Above and opposite: Grand Canyon National Park, Flickr.

Men and nature must work hand in hand. The throwing out of balance of the resources of nature throws out of balance also the lives of men.

—Franklin Delano Roosevelt, January 24, 1935

The CCC: A young man's opportunity to work, to live, to learn, to build and to protect our natural resources. *The National Museum of Forest Service History, forestservicemuseum.org.*

Grand Canyon National Park, South Rim Trail. The CCC helped construct streets and roads, trails, picnic shelters, campgrounds and telephone lines for the Grand Canyon and other national parks. The poignant words from a former CCC member are inscribed on a sign along the Rim Trail at the South Rim: "Maybe those mountains are hard to climb. Those trees are so hard to cut. But the air is pure, the water fine. And we're climbing right out of the rut....For besides helping ourselves, you see, we are helping Mother and Dad." *Swirlyland*.

My grandfather's CCC camp worked to create the LaCreek National Wildlife Refuge in South Dakota. They built the levees, roads, boundary fence and an observation tower; they planted shrubs, trees and marsh plants. Today, this 16,410-acre sanctuary within the semi-arid Great Plains landscape provides a habitat for 250 species of birds and 50 other animals.

In the CCC, Grandpa learned how to drive a truck. He learned to type. His CCC camp superintendent noted that my grandfather was "a very good man, competent with truck and tractor operation." His CCC company commander also noted that he was "a very fine, good man."

Grandpa Lofthouse was honorably discharged from the CCC on April 26, 1937, after securing employment at an automotive firm in Chicago.

The CCC also provided reading education to men who previously were illiterate. Over fifty-seven thousand men in the camps learned to read. Co. 544, CCC, Yellowstone Park in Fort Missoula District, Montana. *National Archives at College Park, Maryland.*

The rest is history: Russell Lofthouse would work as a tool and die maker in Chicago until his retirement. He would raise seven children, including my mother, Barbara.

Most agreed that the CCC was a smashing success. Nearly 3 million men were put to work. In its nine years of existence, the CCC built 125,000 miles of roads, 46,854 bridges and 3,000 lookout fire towers. The CCC enrollees installed over 89,000 miles of telephone wires. They planted over 3 billion trees. The money they sent home to their families uplifted their hometowns' economies.

The New Deal era came to a close in the late 1930s as World War II loomed on the horizon. As the United States mobilized the economy for the war effort, the Great Depression ground to a halt. When the country instituted the Selective Training and Service Act of 1940, requiring all men between the ages of twenty-one and forty-five to register for the draft, the need for work relief declined, and Congress voted to close the Civilian Conservation Corps.

THE CULINARY HISTORY OF THE CIVILIAN CONSERVATION CORPS

We cannot always build the future for our youth,
but we can build our youth for the future.
—*Franklin Delano Roosevelt, January 20, 1937*

For many CCC enrollees like my grandfather, three of the work relief program's main draws were the three meals a day served in the camp mess hall.

The average enrollee was underweight and stood at a below-average height due to malnourishment. He weighed 147 pounds and was 5 feet, 8¼ inches tall.

Enrollee Otis Miller wrote, "We were about 100 pounds when we went in there. It wasn't long before we gained 15 pounds apiece. You could eat a full meal there....You'd eat until you couldn't wiggle. Everyone got rosy-faced and gained weight."

Enrollee Charles Bartell Loomis noted the myriad benefits of the CCC: "Instead of holding down a park bench or pounding the pavements looking for work, today I have work, plenty of good food and a view of the sort that people pay money to see."

CCC enrollees tended to put on weight in the first four weeks at camp, thanks to hearty, nutritious meals. They grew an average of half an inch in height, too, a growth spurt likely spurred on by finally having their nutritional needs met on a more consistent basis. For many of the enrollees, these were the most bountiful meals they'd ever encountered.

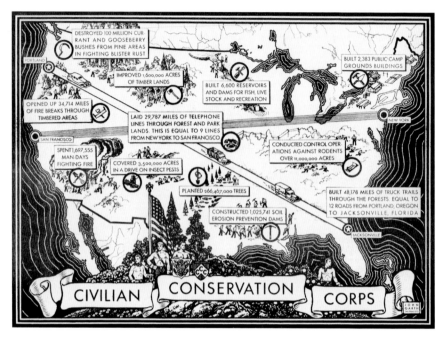

A few of the many Civilian Conservation Corps achievements, depicted by artist John Garth, San Francisco, 1935. *The National Museum of Forest Service History, forestservicemuseum.org.*

"The food itself was wonderful, really wonderful," noted enrollee George Haas (CCC Camp 288, Fort Hancock, Camp Lowe, New Jersey, 1935–38).

"We were so poor when we left home," said enrollee Bill Stangl (CCC Camp NP-3). He continued,

> *I didn't know what a grapefruit looked like until I came to the CCC camp....I never saw pancakes before....I didn't know how to eat a grapefruit. I saw an orange, but I never saw a grapefruit. And breakfast....I never ate breakfast. All I had in my life before I came to the CCC was a cup of coffee and a piece of bread. My mom used to bake her own bread, you know, and a cup of coffee, that's all. But I came into the CCC, golly! This thing was, you know, the quantity of tables lined up with different kinds of foods. So we chowed down pretty good here. They were all good meals.*

Indeed, the official *Thirty Day Menus and Tested Special Recipes for CCC Companies*, prepared by the School for Bakers and Cooks of the Fourth Corps Area, a supplement to the Manual of Mess Management (1939), contains

Top: CCC Company 556 cooks in action, Pokagon State Park, Indiana. *Courtesy of Pokagon State Park.*

Bottom: Grizzly Camp kitchen, Civilian Conservation Corps in Idaho Collection. *Digital Initiatives, University of Idaho Library.*

rich, mouthwatering recipes such as fried ham with gravy, oven roasted turkey with "snowflake" potatoes, fried chicken and baked beans, anchored by vitamin-rich, vegetable-based recipes, including candied carrots, string beans with tomato sauce and cabbage apple slaw. Dessert was always served at dinner, and the CCC mess hall chefs whipped up chocolate cake with fudge frosting, mincemeat cupcakes, apple brown betty, every type of pie under the sun—from blackberry to coconut cream—and cookies galore. Enrollees spoke highly of the meals.

"I wish I could spend a couple of months here myself," said FDR when visiting the Big Meadow CCC Camp, Shenandoah National Park, on August 12, 1933. "The only difference between us is that I am told you men have to put on an average of twelve pounds each. I am trying to lose twelve pounds.…I have seen the boys themselves, and all you have to do is look at them to see that the camps are a success."

CCC Company 556's kitchen force, standing before the camp's Mess Hall, 1935. *The National Museum of Forest Service History, forestservicemuseum.org.*

The CCC-built Juniper picnic area CCC shelter at Theodore Roosevelt National Park, North Dakota. "With little more than strong backs, shovels, and picks, the CCC built roads, trails, culverts, and structures," says the park's website. *Acroterion*.

Working on labor-intensive outdoor projects meant CCC enrollees burned more than four thousand calories a day, so food was an essential fuel.

"It is a well-recognized fact that variety is a most important factor in determining a suitable diet," said Major General J.L. DeWitt, the quartermaster general and brains behind *Subsistence Menus and Recipes for Feeding 100 Men for One Month, Prepared by the Quartermaster Corps Subsistence School* (Chicago, 1933).

> *The human body is not a machine for which energy producing materials can be supplied with mathematical precision. Therefore the physiological and psychological reactions must be taken into consideration, and in order to obtain, in terms of energy, the full value of the ration fed, it must be of such a nature as to appeal to these men and be eaten in sufficient quantity. A monotonous, unattractive, and tasteless meal, while containing a sufficient number of calories and in a sense providing adequate nourishment, may still have a marked adverse influence upon the efficacy of the man through its effect upon his morale. Variety plus quantity plus bulk prepared in an attractive and tasteful manner will do more than all else to keep up morale which is just as essential in these young men as in the soldier.*

Several CCC enrollees pose for a photo with a dead porcupine. The man holding the dead animal is wearing gloves. *Digital Initiatives, University of Idaho Library.*

Kitchen Police's Lament

For I'm peeling with tears in my eyes
'Cause the onions are ripe and new,
Peeling for this hungry crew;
When it's spuds they need for the stew.
Tryin' to smile—once in a while.
But I find it so hard to do,
For I'm peeling with tears in my eyes,
'Cause the onions are ripe and new.

Enrollee Joseph E. Trembley, Company 143, Irving, Massachusetts

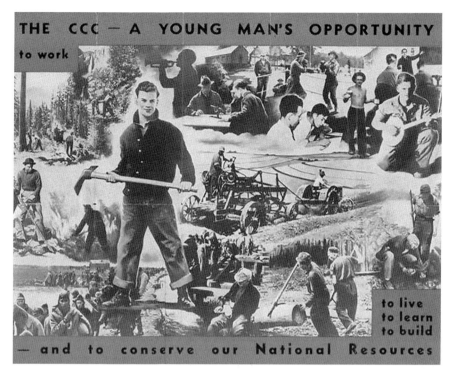

The CCC: A young man's opportunity to work, to live, to learn, to build and to protect our natural resources. *The National Museum of Forest Service History, forestservicemuseum.org.*

Most CCC camps held up to two hundred enrollees and were run by the U.S. Army (unless it was a smaller side or spike camp, which the Forest Service ran for remote projects). Wooden buildings or large tents housed the young men, but the mess hall was usually a permanent structure. Meals were served in the mess hall three times a day unless the enrollees were out in the field, at which point a sack lunch was served or a cook traveled to the field to cook on-site.

The mess hall kitchen was run by both paid staff and enrollees. A junior officer was usually detailed as a mess officer; enrollees assisted in the kitchen. "Cooking and baking are trades in which efficiency depends eighty percent on practical experience," noted the *Thirty Day Menus and Tested Special Recipes for CCC Companies*, prepared by the School for Bakers and Cooks of the Fourth Corps Area. "Every cook should get the proper groundwork and build thereon by practical experience. Cooking is not difficult. Any person of average intelligence can cook a satisfactory meal,

Riverside Walk to Zion Narrows, Zion Canyon, Zion National Park, Utah. Utah's Zion National Park notes on its website, "The CCC built and improved many of Zion Canyon's trails, created parking areas, fought fires, helped build campgrounds, built park buildings, and reduced flooding of the Virgin River." *Ken Lund.*

provided he takes an interest and follows a recipe. The pleasant task of cooking becomes doubly interesting to the cook who is not satisfied with merely cooking well but takes every opportunity of finding new and pleasing ways to prepare foods."

Mess officers had the freedom to create their own camp menus so long as they stayed within the initial budget of forty-five to fifty cents per day per enrollee. The menus show that the mess officers worked hard to provide nutritious, well-rounded meals featuring tasty dishes that the CCC enrollees came to love. They went out of their way to craft delightfully decadent holiday menus, too, still managing to stick mostly within budget. In return, they improved the health of countless young American men. "In making a menu, it is best to bear in mind that in the course of a day, the men should have a balanced diet," suggested *Thirty Day Menus*.

I welcome the opportunity to extend, through the medium of the columns of *Happy Days*, a greeting to the men who constitute the Civilian Conservation Corps. Congratulations are due to those responsible for the successful accomplishment of the gigantic task of creating the camps, arranging for the enlistments, and launching the greatest peacetime movement this country has ever seen.

It is my belief that what is being accomplished will conserve our natural resources, create future national wealth and prove of moral and spiritual value not only to those of you who are taking part, but to the rest of the country as well.

You young men who are enrolled in this work are to be congratulated as well. It is my honest conviction that what you are doing in the way of constructive service will bring to you, personally and individually, returns the value of which it is difficult to estimate. Physically fit, as demonstrated by the examinations you took before entering the camps, the clean life and hard work in which you are engaged cannot fail to help your physical condition and you should emerge from this experience strong and rugged and ready for a re-entrance into the ranks of industry, better equipped than before.

Opportunities for employment in work for which individually you are best suited are increasing daily and you should emerge from this experience splendidly equipped for the competitive fields of endeavor which always mark the industrial life of America.

I want to congratulate you on the opportunity you have and to express to you my appreciation for the hearty cooperation which you have given this movement which is so vital a step in the Nation's fight against the depression and to wish you all a pleasant, wholesome and constructively helpful stay in the woods.

—Franklin Delano Roosevelt, July 8, 1933

The function of food is to furnish energy, build and repair the body, and keep it in a state of health, and to do this, one must have a variety of foods, i.e., milk, meat, cereals, starchy vegetables, bulky vegetables, fruits, and sweets of some kind. Raw salads furnish vitamins that may be destroyed in other foods by the cooking.

It has been noted that men too frequently eat an unbalanced diet of meat, bread, and potatoes. This is an expensive diet, as it requires meat in excessive quantities to satisfy their hunger, where if meat is eaten in conjunction with fruits and vegetables and a satisfying dessert, the cost of the meal is cut, and at the same time the health of the men will be improved. Therefore, in preparing a menu, watch carefully to give a variety of foods in the course of the day. If there is a preponderance of starches one day, cut down on this item the next day, and increase the fruits and bulky vegetables.

The official emblem of the CCC. *The National Museum of Forest Service History, forestservicemuseum.org.*

The official CCC handbook, which every enrollee received, *Your CCC: A Handbook for Enrollees* (1933), included a chapter that outlined the CCC culinary experience, titled, "The Food You Eat":

Food in the CCC is purchased, prepared and served as to give enrollees substantial, healthful, and body-building meals. While there may be an absence of "fancy dishes," few American homes serve meals as scientifically selected as those served at CCC camps.

The CCC menu is the result of many years of experimenting by the U.S. Army, to find the most healthful food values. All food served in the CCC camps is purchased under rigid regulations which require pure and high-grade products. All foods must measure up to U.S. Army standards.

A large part of CCC food, mostly stable produce, is purchased through the Army Quartermaster Corps. Perishable foods are purchased, for the most part, by company or district commanders from food dealers near camps. All meats served in the CCC must pass rigid inspection by Army officers qualified in this work, or by Department of Agriculture meat inspectors.

Food for one man, for one day, is known as a RATION. A definite amount of money is allotted for the purchase of CCC rations. This ration allowance averages between forty-five and fifty cents. This means that each man's food for one day costs that much. Each company is allowed rations for the number of men in the company at a specific time.

CCC kitchen crew. *Gerald W. Williams Collection, OSU Special Collections & Archives, Flickr.*

The food account and supplies in each camp are carefully checked and accounted for by the company commander and are the subject of regular checks by Army inspectors. This is to assure the best possible food for the men and to maintain a strict economy in the purchase and preparation of food.

CCC cooks and bakers are selected for their previous experience in cooking or baking, or learn the trade while in camp. The Army conducts schools for student cooks and bakers, and some camps include cooking and baking in their educational program. Many enrolled have the opportunity of working up from "kitchen police" to positions as cooks.

The mess steward manages the camp kitchen under direction of the company commander. The first cook, or cooks, is the boss of the kitchen. Menus are made several days in advance. The mess steward's job is that of supervising the kitchen, mess hall, and storeroom. Cooking and baking is divided between the first and second cooks and assistant cooks. "Kitchen police" wash pots and pans, prepare vegetables for cooking, and keep the kitchen and mess hall clean. In some camps, they also serve as waiters.

It is my hope that readers will attempt to relive history through these CCC recipes, which I adapted for today's home kitchen or mess hall. All of the featured recipes appeared on CCC camp menus. Budget friendly, with ingredients that can easily be found if not in your very own pantry then at your local grocer, these recipes reflect the "make-do" attitude of Depression-era home cooks. Large-batch recipes can literally feed an army or inexpensively cater a gathering or celebration for friends and family.

These are the recipes that sustained our grandparents and great-grandparents during the Great Depression. All of them offer a taste of a challenging era and a defining moment in U.S. history.

BREAKFAST

CCC camps across the country followed a relatively standard daily routine. Reveille was at 6:00 a.m., and enrollees rushed to wash and dress in their uniforms by 6:30 a.m. They donned either CCC-issued blue denim work or fatigue suits, brown socks, brown handkerchiefs and, weather depending, pea jackets or long overcoats.

After a half hour of calisthenics and a flag-raising ceremony, they trooped off to the mess hall, where they enjoyed a warm breakfast at long tables that sat six to twelve men each. Breakfasts served in CCC mess halls were hearty and delicious, giving the enrollees the energy they needed for a full day of hard work.

The workday began at 7:45 a.m., when the enrollees formed up in rough platoons for roll call and inspection before walking or riding to work, depending on how far the project was from the camp. They worked in small groups under an enrollee leader, doing everything from building trails to lookout towers to footbridges. They installed telephone lines, fought forest fires, planted trees and constructed roads. The work assignments varied from park to park and sometimes from day to day.

Breakfast is the hardest of the three meals for which to prepare menus. Generally speaking, when a heavy meal is to be prepared, four items must be provided: (1) a fruit, fresh or cooked; (2) a cereal, dry or cooked; (3) eggs or a meat dish; (4) toast bread, fritter or doughnuts. An option dish will be potatoes in some form.

The CCC built several trails still in use today at Big Bend National Park, Texas. *Yinyan Chen*.

Fresh fruit may be served three or four times per week, depending on what is available or in season. Fruits include apples, oranges, bananas, melons, peaches, pears (if reasonable in price), and grapes. (Grapefruit are good if relished).

Cooked fruits include stewed, evaporated apples, peaches, apricots, and prunes. The latter, if cooked with stick cinnamon, is much improved. Fried apples are much relished.

Dry cereals are simply served and inexpensive. A number of tests, conducted independently, have shown that it costs less to serve the individual packages than from the proud packages. The small packages cost only about 1¾ cents each.

Cooked cereals include oatmeal, mush (also sometimes fried), boiled rice, Wheatena and Cream of Wheat, and others. Most of these may be improved by the addition of raisins or sliced bananas added when the cereal is two-thirds cooked.

Now comes the expensive item of the four. Eggs are generally served fried, though scrambled eggs and omelets are good for variety. The method of baking eggs in the oven is not good. The cost of two eggs at 30 cents per dozen will

The CCC-built Lost Mine Trail at Big Bend National Park, Texas. The CCC crew arrived at Texas Canyons State Park in 1934 and built trails, roads and other structures that led the park to be declared a national park in 1944. *Yinyan Chen.*

be 5 cents per serving. So this is added to the cost of the cereal and milk; nearly 6 cents makes a total of 11 cents and a big hole in the ration allowance. One-fourth of a pound of bacon per man is as expensive as the eggs.

Sausage is somewhat cheaper than eggs or bacon. Obviously, eggs or bacon can not be served every meal. Now for substitutes more reasonable in price.

Creamed beef made of ground beef leftovers in a cream or brown gravy is good. Ham, pork, or veal may be used instead. When hotcakes or bananas or pineapple fritters are served, potatoes in some form may be added and the meat or eggs dispensed with. Doughnuts may be used in place of the hotcakes or fritters.

The following arrangement is suggested: Eggs twice a week; bacon or sausage once; creamed beef twice; hotcakes once, and fritters or doughnuts for the other day. This will give a variety in the breakfast menu which is much to be desired.

Thirty Day Menus and Tested Special Recipes for CCC Companies, *prepared by the School for Bakers and Cooks of the Fourth Corps Area*

But First, Coffee!

Coffee combines the power of caffeine with a hint of home's comforts and was a key component of breakfast at CCC camps.

It has long played a role in the morale of U.S. soldiers. During the Civil War, a single Union soldier consumed around thirty-six pounds of coffee per year.

By World War I, the U.S. War Department had established local roasting and grinding plants in France so that soldiers had access to a fresh cup of joe. "Coffee was as important as beef and bread…restoring courage and strength," a high-ranking army official concluded postwar.

Instant coffee became widely available in 1910, thanks to the George Washington Coffee Refining Company of Brooklyn, New York, established in 1910, purveyors of instant coffee granules named "Red E Coffee." By the start of World War I, soluble coffee was notably used on the front lines. Soldiers nicknamed it "a cup of George." In a letter from the front, one soldier wrote, "There is one gentleman I am going to look up first after I get through helping whip the Kaiser, and that is George Washington, of Brooklyn, the soldiers' friend."

CCC enrollees take a break for a hot lunch, Cleveland National Forest, California. *The National Museum of Forest Service History, forestservicemuseum.org.*

Sliding Sands Trail, Haleakala National Park, Maui, Hawaii. The park's website notes that along with working to remove invasive plants and feral animals such as pigs and goats, CCC crews constructed the White Hill, Sliding Sands and Halemauu Trails and built some of the structures that are still in use today. *Forrest and Kim Starr, Flickr.*

Oh, the coffee that they serve you they say is mighty fine
It heals cuts and bruises and tastes like iodine.
I don't want no more of the CCC, gee I wanna go home.
The biscuits in the mess hall are said to taste divine
But one rolled off the table and killed a pal of mine.
I don't want no more of the CCC, gee I wanna go home.
The wages that they pay you can buy you paradise.
They last for just one roll of a barrack's game of dice.
I don't want no more of the CCC, gee I wanna go home.
The room and board are furnished along with army clothes
And when I get back home I will have no more such woes.
Oh, I don't want no more of the CCC, gee I wanna go home.

—CCC Camp Gays Mills, Wisconsin's newspaper, the *Kikapoojian*

Both instant and fresh, coffee was so popular among soldiers that the U.S. military even leased a small roasting plant in Paris so that beans could be roasted and ground and expressed to the front lines.

By the time the Armistice was signed on November 11, 1918, the army was roasting 750,000 pounds of green coffee every day and 37,000 pounds of soluble coffee a day. It's no surprise that coffee had extended beyond the front lines after World War I. The United States was the top coffee buyer in the world.

Coffee was an essential element of breakfast at CCC camps across the country.

The CCC, in conjunction with the National Forest Service, transformed millions of acres of national forests. The accomplishments of "Roosevelt's Tree Army" in reforestation still yield benefits today.

Initially, most CCC camps were assigned to national and state forests, public domain land and a few private forests; later on, additional camps were organized for other state and federal agencies that requested specific work projects. The CCC planted more than three billion trees alone.

Many CCC forestry work projects occurred far away from the main CCC camp. Thus, Director Robert Fechner allowed the widespread use of "side" of "spike" camps near work sites. Side camps usually consisted of ten to twenty men living in tents, with a work supervisor or foreman in charge. This campfire coffee recipe is featured in *Camp Cooking*, a recipe book compiled by the National Museum of Forest Service History.

River Runnin' Coffee

Use a coffee pot or empty 1-pound coffee tin. Fill tin with water to within 1 inch of the top of the tin. Holds 12 cups of water. Put in 1 tablespoon of coffee for each cup.

Set the tin on a red-hot bed of coals and forget about it until it boils.

Take the pot off the coals and add ½ cup of cold water to settle the grounds, or toss in two eggshells to do the same thing.

To clean the inside of the tin, wipe dry with paper towels or a cloth. Use no soap! To reduce soot on the outside of the tin, coat the outside of the tin with soap before putting it on coals. Soot will then wash off, even in cold water.

Graham Nut Muffins

1 cup flour

1 cup graham flour

3 teaspoons baking powder

½ cup sugar

½ cup walnut meats

½ teaspoon salt

1 egg, well beaten

1 cup milk

3 tablespoons melted butter

Preheat the oven to 235 degrees and grease a muffin tin or line with paper muffin cups.

Mix flour, graham flour, baking powder, sugar, walnut meats and salt in a large bowl. Stir in egg, milk and butter. Do not overmix.

Bake the muffins for about 20 minutes, or until golden, and a toothpick inserted in the center comes out cleanly.

Cinnamon Sugar Coffee Cake

Simple and quick, this recipe comes from the third edition of All About Home Baking, *published in 1936 (the original was published in 1933) by the General Foods Corporation, manufacturers of Calumet baking powder, Post cereals and Maxwell House Coffee.*

2 cups flour
2 teaspoons baking powder
¾ teaspoon salt
½ cup sugar
6 tablespoons butter
1 egg
½ cup milk

Topping

2 tablespoons butter
¼ cup sugar
1 tablespoon flour
½ teaspoon cinnamon

Preheat the oven to 400 degrees. Grease a 9-inch cake pan. Sift together the flour, baking powder, salt and sugar in a large bowl. Cut in the butter.

In a small bowl, whisk the egg and milk until light and frothy. Pour the egg mixture into the dry ingredients. Stir well until well combined.

Transfer the dough to the prepared pan. Using floured hands, gently pat it down into one even layer. Brush the top of the coffee cake with melted butter. Then, stir together the sugar, flour and cinnamon for the topping. Sprinkle all over the top of the coffee cake.

Bake for 20 minutes, or until golden and a toothpick inserted in the center comes out cleanly. Let cool for 5 minutes in the pan. Then, gently loosen the sides with a butter knife. Turn out onto a plate and then turn back onto a serving plate.

Cornmeal Mush

Soft yet hearty, cornmeal mush is a truly "comfort" breakfast, best served with milk and maple syrup drizzled on top. Seasonal fruit preserves are another delightful topping.

American colonists learned to make the dish, also known as grits, from the Native Americans, and it quickly became an American staple.

Dress up sweet cornmeal mush with butter, a dash of cinnamon, raisins, maple syrup, brown sugar, peanut butter, jam or fresh berries.

For savory grits, omit the sugar and mix in cheese, bacon (cooked and chopped), caramelized onions, roasted red peppers, tomatoes, scallions or fresh herbs, or top each serving with a fried egg.

2½ cups water
½ cup yellow cornmeal
1 tablespoon sugar
Dash of salt

Combine 2 cups of water and salt in a small saucepan and bring to a boil.

Mix cornmeal with a ½ cup of water in a small bowl. Slowly add the cornmeal mixture to boiling water, stirring constantly. Reduce heat to low; cook 5 minutes or until mixture is thickened.

Pineapple Fritters

Pineapple fritters recall both a doughnut shop apple fritter and an onion ring. Use fresh fruit in the summer and canned fruit when it's not in season. Recipe yields 10–12 fritters.

1½ cups flour

3 tablespoons sugar

1 tablespoon baking powder

1 (20-ounce) can crushed pineapple, drained (or 2 cups fresh pineapple, chopped/crushed)

½ cup milk

1 cup canola oil for deep frying

Whisk together flour, sugar and baking powder. Add crushed pineapple and milk and stir until the dough sticks together. Cover and chill for 2 hours.

Pour oil to a depth of 5 inches into a Dutch oven; heat to 375 degrees.

Drop batter by rounded tablespoonfuls, and fry, in batches, 5 minutes or until golden.

Drain fritters on paper towels. Serve with a sprinkle of powdered sugar.

Pork Sausage Gravy

This simple sausage gravy was adapted from a recipe submitted to Favorite Recipes of the CCC Alumni (Pocahontas State Park, Chesterfield, Virginia) by Minnie and Lester Pollary of Keysville, Virginia, CCC Pocahontas Chapter 124. Serve with flaky homemade biscuits for a classic and hearty breakfast treat.

1 pound sausage

2 tablespoons fat from sausage

2 tablespoons flour

1 cup milk

½ teaspoon salt

⅛ teaspoon pepper

Crumble sausage, brown, drain and set aside. In the same skillet, add flour slowly to fat; add milk, stirring constantly until thick. Cook for 5 more minutes. Season with salt and pepper and add drained sausage.

Hanging just outside the mess hall door was a triangular-shaped device made by bending a large steel rod. When the meal was ready, a cook, using another piece of steel rod, would hammer on it and ring the chow call.

Every morning at breakfast, on the table, there would be a large pitcher of milk with small boxes of cereal for each place. Evidently, some of the boys had never been served cereal. They treated it as if it were dessert and ate it last. But, if you ate yours first, as people normally do, when you reached for the ham and eggs, there might not be any left. Some of us organized what we called the "last table gang" and enjoyed our cereal first and then our ham and eggs. Also, on each table, of course, there would be a large pitcher of coffee.

—Frank Davis, CCC Company 411

Three-Ingredient Bread

Made with only three ingredients, this dense bread has a thick, tough crust and keeps fresh longer than other loaves. This recipe yields seven loaves of bread.

You can also freeze your loaves, and they'll stay fresh for up to six months: Wrap each individual loaf tightly in plastic wrap, then wrap again in foil or freezer paper.

1 (5-pound) bag all-purpose flour
3 tablespoons salt
5 tablespoons yeast
6 cups warm water

Pour flour and salt into a large mixing bowl and make a well at its center. Add yeast to the well, and then add about a half cup of the warm water to dissolve the yeast.

Once the yeast is dissolved, slowly add more water, mixing until you form a ball of dough. Knead dough for about three minutes, cover with a dry dish towel and let rise in a warm place.

After the dough has doubled in size, punch down the dough and shape it into 7 loaves. Let the loaves rise for another hour. Place each loaf in a greased 9-inch loaf pan.

Bake at 350 degrees until the loaves get brown on top, about 25 minutes (this will vary a bit based on your oven).

Food in the CCC generally was excellent. My first meal in a 3C's mess hall was a memorable one for a depression kid to whom food was dear. I ate enough for three men. There were eight of us seated at a table, family-style. As soon as a dish or platter was emptied, it was refilled again until we had eaten as much as we wanted.

I was amazed at the variety and amount of food placed on a table for eight men to consume. In those lean years, I had not known such food existed! And that first meal was typical: braised sirloin tips, vegetables, including tomatoes and potatoes, Waldorf salad, apples and nuts, bread and butter, orange marmalade, and ice cream for dessert.

The diet was calculated to supply the necessary minerals and vitamins for a healthy body, and was prepared by capable CCC cooks under the watchful eyes of a mess sergeant, usually an enrollee especially trained for that duty.

A former mess sergeant recalled, "I fed each man on thirty-nine cents a day; we didn't throw anything away."

The structured lifestyle of the CCC—work, sleep, exercise, and fresh air—gave us tremendous appetites. For the first time in our lives, we had all the food we could want.

—Edwin Hill, CCC corps member, at Camp Hard Labor Creek in Shenandoah, Georgia. Excerpt from his memoir, *In the Shadow of the Mountain* (Pullman: Washington State University Press, 1990)

Moonstruck Toast

If you've ever made an egg-in-a-hole—an egg cracked inside a slice of bread—you know it's easy, tasty and, most importantly, fun. But why have your egg on top of your toast when you could have it nestled inside? For those with a sweet tooth, toast may also be topped with maple syrup or fresh fruit jam. Adapted from a recipe submitted to Favorite Recipes of the CCC Alumni *(Pocahontas State Park, Chesterfield, Virginia) by Carol M. Adams of Richmond, Virginia, CCC Pocahontas Chapter 124.*

2 strips thick-sliced bacon
1 thick slice French or Italian bread
1 egg
Butter
Salt and pepper to taste
Maple syrup or fresh fruit jam (optional)

Fry bacon slowly until crispy. Set aside.

Scoop out a circular hole in the center of thickly sliced bread, large enough to hold an egg. Melt a small amount of butter in the skillet on medium-high heat (or use a bit of leftover bacon grease). Place bread in a skillet and crack the egg into the center hole. Allow bread to brown on one side, then flip over and brown the other side until the egg is cooked to desired consistency.

Remove from skillet, salt and pepper to taste, crisscross the top with bacon and serve.

Mealtime at CCC Camp
Roosevelt, George Washington
National Forest, Virginia. *USFS
photo, Gerald W. Williams Collection.*

KELLOGG'S AND THE CCC

Dr. John Harvey Kellogg had an unparalleled zeal for wellness with a passion for health reform. With his trademark white suit and white shoes and, at times, a white cockatoo perched on his shoulder for extra zest, his beliefs—many of which he claimed arrived as "visions"—he is widely considered the nation's first "celebrity doctor" thanks to his many renowned patients, among them Thomas Edison, Henry Ford, Amelia Earhart and several U.S. presidents, including Herbert Hoover.

Today, Kellogg's health advice is considered downright quackery: at his holistic wellness clinic, the Battle Creek Sanitarium, he prescribed days-long soaks in a bathtub to cure everything from diarrhea to mania. He was a proponent of super enemas, pumping up to fifteen quarts of water per minute into patients' bowels. He believed that the "vile practice" of masturbation led to poor digestion, epilepsy and even insanity and recommended treatment with circumcision without anesthetic.

"A man that lives on pork, fine-flour bread, rich pies and cakes, and condiments, drinks tea and coffee, and uses tobacco, might as well try to fly as to be chaste in thought," he wrote in his (1881) tome *Plain Facts for Old and Young*, and his sanitarium served strictly vegetarian meals.

Corn flakes breakfast cereal, originally made with wheat, was created at the Battle Creek Sanitarium as a breakfast option by Dr. John Harvey's brother, Will Kellogg, in 1894. The brothers battled over the patent, with John Harvey preferring to keep the cereal as an exclusive product served only to the sanitarium's patients, but Will won and launched the Battle Creek Toasted Corn Flake Company in 1906. In 1922, the company took on its current name, the Kellogg Company, popularly known as Kellogg's.

In 1931, the Home Economics Department of Kellogg Company formed a partnership with the armed forces. The company created a range of menus and recipes for the U.S. Army at Fort Sheridan, Illinois. Later, the program was expanded to include units of the Marine Corps, Navy, Coast Guard, National Guard and, eventually, the CCC.

The Kellogg Company was the only cereal maker to call on the CCC camps during the agency's first year (1933). Some Kellogg Company sales representatives reportedly drove more than one thousand miles each week to reach camps located in dense forests and mountainous regions across the nation, ensuring that they were well-supplied with Kellogg's cereals.

Aalii plants along the trail near Holua Cabin, Haleakala National Park, Maui, Hawaii. The CCC built some of Maui's Haleakala National Parkpark's most iconic features through the volcanic terrain. *Forrest and Kim Starr, Flickr.*

The most popular building in the camp was the mess hall. It was staffed by two teams of cooks who worked on alternate days, "K.P.s" (Kitchen Police, of course). Their hours were from around four o'clock in the morning until eight o'clock in the evening. Since our electrical power plant had been shut down at ten o'clock the previous evening their first job was to start it again in the morning.

Early one morning, and I mean early, I was awakened by one of the cooks who asked me to go out and start the power plant. Knowing where my next meal was coming from, I, of course, complied. They had been unable to get the power going. The weather was very, very cold, and they had flooded the engine with gasoline. I removed the spark plugs, squirted some oils in the cylinders to establish compression, and got the engine started and the electric lights working.

I walked back into the candle-lit kitchen and was greeted by a round of applause. I was told that I could have anything that I wanted to eat. I said, "How about some scrambled eggs?" The cook said, "How many do you want?" I said, "How many do you have?" I think I ate somewhere between a half and a whole dozen. For once in my life I was full.

—Frank Davis, CCC Company 411

CASH PRIZES for C.C.C. Men!

LOOK AT THESE PRIZES!

FIRST PRIZE
$50⁰⁰

SECOND PRIZE
$20⁰⁰

THIRD PRIZE $10⁰⁰
NEXT SIX PRIZES . . (EACH) $5⁰⁰
NEXT TWENTY PRIZES (EACH) $2⁰⁰

Enter any time before June 1st
Read these simple rules:

1 Contest is open only to men of the Civilian Conservation Corps.

2 Write plainly on one side of a sheet of white paper, telling in 100 words or less "Why I like Kellogg's Wheat Krispies."

3 Mail your contest letter to Dept. C, Kellogg Company, Battle Creek, Mich., not later than midnight, June 1, 1935.

4 Letters will be judged solely on a basis of their clear, convincing quality. In case of a tie, duplicate prizes will be awarded.

5 The decisions of the judges shall be final.

6 All letters submitted in this contest become the property of the Kellogg Company.

All right ... let's go!

HERE'S a prize contest that will bring real money to men of the Civilian Conservation Corps. Twenty-nine liberal cash prizes — and they're easy to win, because this contest is *limited to members of the C.C.C.*

The Kellogg Company has recently brought out a remarkable new ready-to-eat cereal — Kellogg's Wheat Krispies. It's on the menu for morning mess at all camps. Perhaps you've tried it already, and discovered the amazing new *crispness* that Kellogg has given whole wheat by blending with rice. Wheat Krispies *stay* crisp in milk. And they have a tempting flavor you've never found before in any wheat cereal.

We want every C.C.C. man to try Kellogg's Wheat Krispies. We want to know what you think of them. And for that information we're offering $150 in cash prizes! *Nothing to buy. No package tops to send!*

Eat a bowl of Wheat Krispies. Then get out your pencil and jot down some of the reasons why *you* like them. Write your reasons in 100 words or less, simply and clearly, without literary frills. Then mail us the letter. That's all! It's a cinch!

Kellogg's
WHEAT KRISPIES

In 1931, the Home Economics Department of Kellogg Company launched a cooperative effort with the armed forces with demonstrations of possible menus for the U.S. Army at Fort Sheridan, Illinois. The program was expanded to include the CCC, plus menu services and cooking demonstrations for units of the Marine Corps, Navy, Coast Guard and National Guard. *Kellogg's.*

Good health and morale are the greatest assets an organization can have. Both are influenced more by the quality of the mess than by any other factor. A balanced and varied diet of good food, well cooked and attractively served, is the foundation of a successful camp.

These menus and recipes have been tested and found practical. They are intended as a guide only and are sent to you with the hope that the difficult task of menu planning may be made easier.

KELLOGG COMPANY

Battle Creek, Michigan

C-4

Kellogg Company was the only cereal maker to call on the CCC camps during the agency's first year (1933). Some Kellogg Institution Division sales representatives reportedly drove more than one thousand miles each week to reach camps located in backcountry and mountainous locations across the nation, ensuring that they were well-supplied with Kellogg's cereals. *Kellogg's.*

"Good health and morale are the greatest assets an organization can have," reads the introduction to a Kellogg Company CCC recipe booklet.

Both are influenced more by the quality of the mess than by any other factor. A balanced and varied diet of good food, well cooked and attractively served, is the foundation of a successful camp. The larger amount of food cooked at one time, the more difficult to season well and to retail the "home flavor."…The greatest difficulty is to supply varied and appetizing meals without utilizing unusual foods and flavors. Service men like plain food, well cooked and moderately seasoned, which is filling and satisfying. They like dishes to which they are accustomed, but they dislike monotony. When you realize that these individuals have come from different climates, from widely separated areas, from homes in which the environment may have been good, bad or indifferent, and where food habits probably were influenced by one or more of the countries of Europe, it is not surprising that the food is sometimes exposed to frank criticism. Meals are to be commended which evoke no complaints even though words of praise are few.

Kellogg's created handy cookbooks with menu and recipe suggestions for the Civilian Conservation Corps. It's no surprise that many of the recipes called for Kellogg's products. *Nicky Ball, naturalist, Pokagon State Park, Indiana.*

All-Bran Muffins

The Kellogg Company introduced the high-fiber wheat bran breakfast cereal All-Bran in 1916, touting it as the secret to leading a life "free of constipation."

Thanks to two full cups of All-Bran cereal per recipe, each muffin boasts 14 percent of the recommended daily amount of fiber. For muffins with reduced fat and cholesterol, substitute 2 egg whites for 1 egg and ¼ cup sweetened applesauce or ¼ cup mashed bananas for ¼ cup vegetable oil.

1¼ cups flour
½ cup sugar
1 tablespoon baking powder
¼ teaspoon salt
2 cups Kellogg's All-Bran
1¼ cups fat-free milk
1 egg
¼ cup vegetable oil

Preheat the oven to 400 degrees. Stir together flour, sugar, baking powder and salt. Set aside.

In a mixing bowl, combine cereal and milk. Let stand for about 2 minutes or until cereal softens. Add egg and oil. Beat well.

Add flour mixture, stirring until combined. Fill greased muffin tins two-thirds full and bake for about 20 minutes, or until golden brown.

Citrusade

The Fire Camp Cookbook from 1928 recommends keeping this breakfast refreshment, packed with vitamins, cool by setting the bottle in a creek or spring until ready to serve. The original recipe calls for whipping the ingredients vigorously in a boiler; modern kitchens will want to implement a blender.

1 (15-ounce) can of red grapefruit
12 cups water
¼ cup food-grade powdered citric acid
1 cup sugar

Blend the ingredients in a blender for about two minutes. Keep cool until ready to serve.

There were, I believe, about twenty tables in the mess hall. Some two hundred men were served. Near the exit from the mess hall stood a large screened-in box where the loaf bread was kept. Sometimes during the winter months, on our way out after the evening meal, one of us would snitch a loaf of bread and take it to the barracks, where we would make toast on the wood stove that night.

The bread was delivered every other day by a truck from Asheville. Sometimes when a boy was going back home for any reason, he would hitch a ride to Asheville on the bread truck and take a bus from there. What do they say? "Bread is the staff of life."

—Frank Davis, CCC Company 411

Zwieback

Zwieback is a long-lasting, crisp, sweetened bread, made with eggs and baked twice, hence its name in German: zwei (two) and backen, meaning "to bake," which literally translates to "twice-baked."

Zwieback originated in East Prussia, where it was a staple for soldiers during the Thirty Years' War, and the Mennonites brought the bread to the United States.

1 cup milk	1 tablespoon active dry yeast
4 tablespoons butter	¼ cup warm water
¼ cup honey	1 egg
1 teaspoon salt	4 cups flour
⅔ cup white sugar	Pinch freshly grated nutmeg

In a small saucepan, heat milk until it begins to bubble. Remove from heat; stir in butter, honey and salt. Set aside and let cool. Set aside 2 teaspoons of sugar. Stir the remaining sugar into the milk mixture. Let cool to room temp.

In a separate mixing bowl, combine yeast and lukewarm water. Let sit for 5 minutes while yeast activates. With a whisk, beat cooled milk mixture, egg, 4 cups flour and nutmeg into yeast mixture.

Knead dough in a bowl, adding up to ½ cup more flour if necessary until a smooth, soft dough forms. Divide dough into 8 balls 3 inches in diameter. Place balls 4 inches apart on lightly greased cookie sheets; pat into 4-inch rounds. Brush tops of rounds with water and sprinkle with reserved sugar. Set aside, lightly covered with kitchen towels, about 1 hour, or until doubled in size.

Preheat the oven to 350 degrees. Bake raised rounds 30 minutes or until golden brown. Remove from the oven; leave the oven on. Wait 20 minutes before baking a second time.

Cut each round into six ½-inch slices using a serrated knife. Place slices, cut sides down, on cookie sheets, and return to the oven for 5 minutes. Turn slices and bake 5 minutes longer, or until golden on both sides. Turn off heat and leave in the unopened oven until cool, about 45 minutes. Store well-wrapped, at room temperature.

Mess Hall U.S. CCC C0556 Angola, Indiana 10/24/33 2

Mess Hall, CCC Company 556, Pokagon State Park, Indiana. Indiana's Pokagon State Park is home to one of the largest collections of remaining Civilian Conservation Corps structures in Indiana. While at Pokagon, Company 556 worked on the future park's county road bridge, its beach, bathhouse, saddle barn, gatehouse, CCC shelter, group camp, park office and campgrounds. They also planted hundreds of trees and, during their downtime, created a public attraction still enjoyed today, the Pokagon State Park Toboggan Run. *Courtesy of Pokagon State Park.*

LARGE-BATCH BREAKFAST DISHES

ONE HUNDRED DOUGHNUTS

When it comes to things that go well with coffee, doughnuts are an iconic choice.

Doughnuts were introduced to the United States via Dutch settlers to New Amsterdam. Author Washington Irving mentioned them in his 1809 *History of New York* as "balls of sweetened dough, fried in hog's fat, and called dough-nuts, or *olykoeks*."

In 1917, the Salvation Army sent 250 volunteers to France to boost morale by handing out clothing, supplies and doughnuts to U.S. soldiers. The volunteers earned the sweet nickname "Doughnut Dollies." Volunteer Margaret Sheldon wrote of one busy day: "Today I made 22 pies, 300 doughnuts, 700 cups of coffee." In 1938, the Salvation Army declared June 4 National Doughnut Day to honor the Doughnut Dollies.

This recipe yields a whopping one hundred doughnuts. Though they taste delicious plain, they can also be served sprinkled with powdered sugar or dusted with cinnamon and sugar.

If you have extras, store in the freezer—they should stay fresh there for two to three months—in sealed, heavy-duty freezer bags; leave uncovered on the counter for fifteen minutes to defrost them.

FRENCH TOAST FOR ONE HUNDRED

French toast was first mentioned in *Apicius*, a collection of Latin recipes dating to the first century CE, where it's described as *aliter dulcia*, "another sweet dish." This easy recipe works with many types of bread—white, whole wheat, sourdough, Italian or French—and is an excellent way to make use of stale bread.

We were ushered from the railroad car and into a mess hall where we were given doughnuts and coffee. We were then assigned the tents in which we were to live for the next two weeks. We were quartered, six men to a tent, with folding army cots and straw tick mattresses to sleep on. The next morning, we were given another and more detailed physical examination.

We were issued mess kits, and our meals were served in the mess hall. The cooks wore white shirts and pants and large white chef's hats. The food they served was good. It consisted of such things as ham and eggs, cereal, and milk and coffee to drink. The boys would eat until all the food was gone. I would sometimes go back for seconds and thirds in the chow line.

One day, the mess sergeant said to me, "Boy, don't you ever get enough to eat?" I answered, "Not that I can remember." Outside the mess hall, there was a steel drum filled with water where we could wash our mess kits.

—Frank Davis, CCC Company 411

One Hundred Doughnuts

1½ cups butter
1½ pounds sugar
1 tablespoon vanilla extract
10 eggs
5 tablespoons baking powder
20 cups flour
3 cups water
Canola oil for deep frying

Cream the butter and sugar: Start with room-temperature butter and beat at a low speed, until the butter is creamy and whipped. Add the sugar and beat on high until fluffy. Add the vanilla extract. Beat the eggs well and then beat them into the creamed butter and sugar.

Sift the baking powder and flour together and add to the creamed butter, sugar and eggs. Add the water and stir until the dough is smooth.

Roll out to the thickness of about ½ inch and cut with a doughnut cutter. If no doughnut cutter is on hand, cut out into pieces about 2 inches wide by 3 inches long and form a doughnut shape.

Heat oil to 360 degrees and gently drop rounds into the oil in batches of 3 to 5 depending on the size of your frying pan. Don't crowd the doughnuts. Fry doughnuts for approximately two minutes on each side or until golden brown. Allow to cool on a wire rack before serving.

Cornmeal Mush for One Hundred

3 tablespoons salt
7 gallons water
3 pounds sugar
10 pounds yellow cornmeal

Bring the salted water to a boil; then add the sugar and cornmeal while stirring briskly to prevent lumps. Cook for about 20 minutes and then allow to stand about the same length of time where it will remain hot. Serve with fresh milk or evaporated milk poured over it.

French Toast for One Hundred

30 pounds bread
5 (12-ounce) cans evaporated milk
14 cups water
10 eggs
5 tablespoons vanilla extract
2¼ cups cornstarch
Salt to taste
Butter for frying

Slice the bread, each slice not more than ½ inch thick. Whip the milk, water, eggs, vanilla extract and cornstarch into a batter. Add salt to taste. Dip slices in the batter and fry in butter on a griddle.

Baking Powder Biscuits for One Hundred

This recipe yields a whopping 300 biscuits, enough to feed an army of 100. Adapted from Subsistence Menus and Recipes for Feeding 100 Men for One Month, *prepared by the Quartermaster Corps Subsistence School, Chicago, Illinois, April 25, 1933.*

15 pounds flour

2½ cups baking powder

6 tablespoons salt

7½ cups butter, room temperature

20 cups milk

Sift the dry ingredients together three times and work in the butter. Make a well in the middle and add all the milk. Stir until mixed. Should make a soft dough; if not, add more milk. Turn out on a lightly floured board and knead quickly for not more than a minute.

The secret to making good biscuits is in handling the dough only enough to mix thoroughly. Roll out to ½ the thickness desired in the baked biscuit, cut out with a biscuit cutter, and place in baking pans just touching each other. Bake at 425 degrees for 12 minutes or until golden brown. Serve hot.

Larry Herron holds the rolling pin his father, Leo Harron, a CCC camp cook, used to roll biscuits. Herron was the first cook for CCC Company 1592, Camp S-93, Bluffton, Indiana (Ouabache State Park). *Shelley Reed, Naturalist, Ouabache State Park, Indiana.*

All-Bran Muffins for One Hundred

6 cups Kellogg's All-Bran

12 cups buttermilk

6 cups sugar

12 tablespoons butter

3 tablespoons salt

9 eggs

11 cups flour

½ cup baking powder

2 tablespoons baking soda

Preheat the oven to 425 degrees. Soak All-Bran in the buttermilk for about five minutes. Cream sugar, butter and salt. Add eggs, one or two at a time, and beat in well. Add All-Bran and buttermilk and mix thoroughly.

Add sifted dry ingredients, stirring as little as possible to mix in the flour. Fill greased muffin tins two-thirds full and bake for 20 minutes, or until golden brown.

LUNCH AND SUPPER

Lunch was served at noon, either delivered to the work site or eaten in the mess hall. An hour was dedicated to lunch, which was oftentimes a rich, hot meal or else hearty sandwiches with pie for dessert. Coffee fueled the day and was served at every meal.

A substantial dinner, or supper, was served at around 5:30 p.m. and always featured meat, a side dish made with fresh vegetables and dessert.

Between the return from the work site at about 4:00 p.m. until the dinner bell rang and during dedicated, post-dinner evening recreational hours, enrollees enjoyed playing football, baseball or basketball—major league scouts were known to recruit from CCC camps—or a casual game of pool or table tennis, depending on the season. Others settled into the camp library, where books by popular authors, including Rex Beach, Sax Rohmer, Rafael Sabatini and Edgar Wallace awaited eager eyes, as well as major newspapers and magazines such as *Life*, *Time*, *Newsweek*, the *Saturday Evening Post*, *Radio News* and the Sears-Roebuck catalogue.

Some enrollees attended classes as part of the camp education program. Some went to the nearest town to catch a movie or, even better, meet a girl. All that mattered was that you were back by 9:45 p.m., when camp lights flashed off and on, the warning signal that in just fifteen minutes, the lights would be turned off. The evening lullaby was taps.

Saturday mornings called for camp maintenance or laundry, but enrollees were largely free on weekends. They staged theatrical productions and

Top: CCC recruits lie in their cots in the barracks at Camp 657 in Elcho, Wisconsin, circa 1933–37. Note the barrel stove, one of three located in the barracks. *Langlade County Historical Society.*

Bottom: The kitchen crew of CCC Camp 818, Phantom Ranch, Grand Canyon National Park. *Grand Canyon National Park, Flickr.*

Opposite: Leo Herron, first cook, CCC Company 1592, Camp S-93, Bluffton, Indiana (Ouabache State Park). *Courtesy of Larry Herron.*

hosted dances and sporting events. Camp trucks carried them into town, where they enjoyed a stroll down Main Street, hand in hand with a local girl if lucky. Boxing matches were popular, as they required little equipment, only two men willing to fight. Religious services were held in all camps on Sundays thanks to a dedicated corps of 154 full-time CCC chaplains on duty. They drafted their very own camp newspapers or contributed to the national CCC newspaper, *Happy Days*.

These truly were "happy days" for so many CCC enrollees.

In preparing the menus for lunch, we must first answer the following question: Is the meal to be sent out, or is it to be served in the dining room? We will consider first meals sent out to working parties, to soldiers on the

rifle or pistol range, or on one-day maneuvers. If it can be possibly avoided, sandwiches should not be furnished to the men at noon. In the summer, the sandwiches dry out and become unpalatable; in the wintertime, they may freeze and thereby become unsatisfactory. Too, the men get to feeling that the ones doing the lighter work around the camp are getting the best of the deal by having hot meals.

The main dish to be sent out for hot lunch may be either one of the steaks, roasts, or stews shown in the recipes. It should include some starchy vegetables, such as potatoes or corn, and a juicy or leafy vegetable, also an easily carried dessert, such as canned fruit or other simple sweets. Coffee may be sent out already prepared and accompanied with sugar and evaporated milk, or it may be prepared in the field through the use of large coffee pots or buckets. This same menu will serve for the lesser number of men who remain behind in the camp.

When all the men are to be fed in the mess hall, a more elaborate meal may be prepared and served.

Thirty Day Menus and Tested Special Recipes for CCC Companies, *prepared by the School for Bakers and Cooks of the Fourth Corps Area*

Spike Camp Cooking

Since many CCC forestry work projects occurred far away from the main CCC camp at so-called side or spike camps near work sites deep within the forests, the U.S. Department of Agriculture Forest Service drafted the Fire Camp Cookbook in 1928, providing clear instructions for setting up an impromptu "mess fire" in the forest.

Upon arriving at the spot selected for the camp, the camp foreman will ordinarily detail two or more men to assist the cook and flunkies in setting up the kitchen.

The kitchen should be located at a point where water can be obtained with the least effort.

The men should, in all cases, be quarter[ed] below the source of water supply.

S if for the stew they always feed us.
H if for the home we seldom see.
O is for the onions and our taste buds.
V is for the coming victory.
E is for the end of our enlistment.
L is for the last you'll see of me.
Put them all together and they spell S-H-O-V-E-L, the symbol of the CCC.

—CCC Camp Gays Mills, Wisconsin's newspaper, the *Kikapoojian*

The first need in a new camp is the open fire. The cook will designate a site for this, and his men will build the fireplace according to the following directions:

Dig a trench about three feet long, 18 inches wide, and a foot deep. This trench should run in the direction of the prevailing wind, which in a valley or creek bottom is generally up or downstream. Cut two small logs about three feet long and six inches in diameter; lay one of these crosswise at each end of the trench, cut two shallow notches about 10 inches apart, near the center of each log, and in these lay the fire irons, which are in two sections and must be screwed together. They will be found in the mess box. Start a good fire the entire length of the trench and turn it over to the cook.

After the open fire is prepared, the tables for work and serving should be built.

The cook's work table should be built first and should be about 8 feet long and 3 feet wide.

The serving table is about 16 feet long and 2½ feet wide.

As everyone will stand when using these tables, they should be higher than ordinary; the length of an ax and handle is a good height.

The work table is built by driving stakes about 3 inches in diameter into the ground for legs, with cross pieces of the same material spiked on top and a cover of small poles laid lengthwise for a temporary top. As fast as empty boxes are available, they can be taken apart and the pieces nailed on top of the poles. A stake about 6 feet long is also driven into the ground at each end of the table near the center. To this is spiked a crossbar extending the entire length of the table and about two feet above it. Nails are driven into this so the cook can hang the different tools and utensils within reach when working.

The serving table is built in the same way, except, if desired, instead of driving stakes in the ground for legs, blocks of wood about 18 inches in diameter set on end may be used.

The Forest Service Fire Camp Cookbook also details the instructions for preparing spike camp sack lunches.

For supper, there should be the following: Soup, a meat dish, some vegetables, a salad, and a baked dessert.

In his day's menu we have now covered the requirements: a baked article for supper, a soup, a salad, and a variety of vegetables.

In planning a menu it should be remembered that there are certain combinations of foods that have been found to complement each other for various reasons—a nice blending of flavors, or a balancing of the diet.

For example, hot cakes, sausage, and sirup are well served together; roast pork, or roast beef and mashed potatoes; lemon with fish; pickles with baked beans; dressings with roast meats and fowl; celery with oysters; tart or piquant foods with fish; cheese with apple pie; sweet potatoes or apple sauce, or stewed apples with roast pork.

Watch carefully in planning your menus that the same food or flavor is not repeated twice in the same meal, i.e., tomato soup and fresh tomato salad; Waldorf salad and apple pie; boiled cabbage and coleslaw, etc.

The making of a menu requires a good deal of thought and can not be passed over lightly.

Thirty Day Menus and Tested Special Recipes for CCC Companies, *prepared by the School for Bakers and Cooks of the Fourth Corps Area*

Sack Lunches for Thirty Men

This lunch is packed in boxes marked "Sack Lunch." Each box contains a complete lunch for thirty men and consists of the following articles:

2 cans sandwich meat or boiled ham

3 pounds cheese

3 cans jam

18 loaves bread or 12 sandwich loaves

30 (8-ounce) cans fruit

1 jar mustard

36 paper lunch sacks

30 paper spoons

2 can openers

1 slicing knife

1 can (2 pounds) butter

Each individual lunch will consist of

2 meat sandwiches

1 cheese sandwich

1 jam

1 can fruit

1 paper spoon

Packed in individual sacks.

Instructions for Preparing

Slice the meat about 4 slices to the inch.

Slice the bread about 4 slices to the inch.

Slice the cheese lengthwise 5 slices to the inch.

Pack the lunch in the sacks for the men with the meat sandwiches on top so they can use mustard on the meat if they so desire.

Left: *Happy Days*, CCC newspaper from April 27, 1935. *Courtesy of the California State Archives.*

Below: Civilian Conservation Corps boys from Camp F-167, Salmon National Forest, Idaho, ready to transplant beaver from a ranch to forest watershed, where they will help conserve water supply. At right is Emmett Steeples, camp superintendent, circa 1938. *FDR Presidential Library & Museum.*

CIVILIAN CONSERVATION CORPS VEGETABLE SOUP

Since moms weren't present to remind their sons, "Eat your vegetables," many CCC camps served vegetable soup as a prelude to lunch and supper. The catch was that you had to eat your bowl of veggie soup before enjoying the rest of your meal. This recipe was adapted to include seasonal vegetables, but the rule of thumb was to include one veggie from aboveground and one veggie from underground. Any leftover meat on hand (bologna, sausage, etc.) can be used to add protein to the soup.

NAVY BEAN SOUP

Navy bean soup is a U.S. original. Made with a variety of the common bean (*Phaseolus vulgaris*) native to the Americas, where it was first domesticated, it's been served by U.S. Navy cooks since the nineteenth century and at U.S. Senate restaurants since the early twentieth century. Cheap and easy to make, it was a CCC mess hall mainstay.

According to the Senate's official website, it was either Senator Fred Dubois of Idaho (in office March 4, 1891–March 3, 1897) or Senator Knute Nelson of Minnesota (in office January 4, 1893–January 31, 1895) who first requested the soup.

The famous soup faced a dilemma during World War II when rationing limited navy bean supply. On September 14, 1943, the Senate kitchen didn't have enough navy beans to serve the soup, an incident so jarring that the *Washington Times-Herald* reported on its absence the following day. In 1988, Senator Bob Dole said of the navy bean shortage, "Somehow, by the next day, more beans were found, and bowls of bean soup have been ladled up without interruption ever since."

CHIPPED BEEF ON TOAST

Cheap, filling and easy to prepare, chipped beef on toast is a classic Depression-era recipe. It's tasty, too. The dish earned its negative nicknames—SOS, which stood for "Save Our Stomachs," "Same Ole Stuff" or, perhaps worst

Cheap, filling and easy to prepare, chipped beef on toast is a classic Depression-era recipe. It's tasty, too. The dish earned its negative nicknames—SOS, which stood for "Save Our Stomachs," "Same Ole Stuff" or, perhaps worst of all, "Shit on a Shingle"—only because it was served up so very often, sometimes on a daily basis, in canteens across the country. Indeed, many CCC former enrollees often craved the dish, recalling it with nostalgia. *Kurt Wagner, Flickr.*

of all, "Shit on a Shingle"—only because it was served up so very often, sometimes daily, in canteens across the country. Indeed, many CCC former enrollees often craved the dish, recalling it with nostalgia. It's the ultimate warm, comforting dish, one that you can count on to fill your belly and provide the energy needed for long hours of hard work. It was often served as a main course for breakfast.

Chipped beef on toast was a cheaper, calorie-rich version of biscuits and gravy. Beef stock, evaporated milk, butter, flour, toast, butter and dried beef are used to make a quick, easy and cheap gravy. The dish's main ingredient, chipped beef, is a form of pressed, salted and dried beef, described by one of its original U.S. producers, Hormel, as "an air-dried product that is similar to bresaola, but not as tasty."

The first appearance of a chipped beef on toast recipe may be in the 1910 *Manual for Army Cooks*. From the army canteen, the dish made its way into CCC canteens and then homes across the country as mothers adopted the inexpensive, hearty dish into their weekly meal planning during the lean Depression years, personalizing the dish by adding spices to the chipped beef gravy and adding garden vegetables to up the nutrient value.

This recipe for army-sized servings of a Depression-era classic was presented by Paul Hull of Company No. 4787 from Burns, Oregon, which he adapted from his 1918 *U.S. Army Cookbook*.

BREAD AND BUTTER PICKLES

Home canning helped families stretch produce during the Depression. Communities set up common canning centers, using their collective force to preserve the fruits of the harvest. "The canning center movement was accelerated by the widespread decrease in farm income and progressive unemployment in towns and cities, which threw millions of people upon the relief rolls," noted the U.S. Department of Agriculture Bureau of Home Economics in 1935.

A bumper crop of cucumbers called for bread and butter pickles, the perfect addition to sandwiches year-round.

Why are they called bread and butter pickles?

Cucumber farmers Omar and Cora Fanning started selling sweet and sour pickles under the trademark "Fanning's Bread and Butter Pickles" in 1923. During lean years, the Fannings survived by making the pickles with their surplus of undersized cucumbers and bartering them with their grocer for staples such as bread and butter.

This recipe is for quick bread and butter pickles, which will stay fresh in your refrigerator for up to two weeks. For safe shelf-stable storage at home, the jars must be hot-water bath processed.

For my first day at work in the CCC camp, I was assigned to the trail crew. Our job was to build fire trails throughout the mountains to give access to firefighters to combat forest fires and build hiking trails for recreational use. At 8:00 a.m., we left the camp and started walking to the job. As the rail progressed, the work area became farther and farther from the camp. On this day, we walked for three hours before reaching the work site. We worked for one hour and then stopped for lunch. Our lunches were brown bags picked up that morning when leaving the mess hall. They were all alike, of course, consisting of a baloney sandwich and a jelly sandwich. Peanut butter and jelly were my favorites, so I traded my baloney sandwich and my cheese sandwich for another peanut butter and another jelly. Putting them together, I had two extra thick peanut butter and jelly sandwiches.

—Frank Davis, Civilian Conservation Corps Company 411

Many CCC forestry work projects occurred far away from the main CCC camp at so-called side or spike camps deep within the forest. *U.S. National Archives and Records Administration.*

A CCC enrollee plants a locust tree, circa mid-1930s. This planting took place as part of a Lexington, Tennessee reforestation project. *FDR Presidential Library & Museum.*

BRUNSWICK STEW

Brunswick stew was a CCC canteen mainstay, typically spiked with easily caught critters such as rabbits or squirrels.

Two states claim to be the birthplace of hearty bean and tomato-based Brunswick stew. A plaque on a large, cast-iron pot in Brunswick, Georgia, claims that the first Brunswick stew was made on nearby St. Simons Island on July 2, 1898.

Meanwhile, Virginia is home to the annual Brunswick stew cook-off contest, where contestants compete for the prestigious title of Brunswick County Stewmaster, while a 1988 state proclamation declared Virginia's Brunswick County to be "the place of origin of this astonishing gastronomic miracle." A Virginia state travel guide, published by the Federal Writers' Project in 1941, remarked:

> *Native to this county is Brunswick Stew, a flavorous brew first concocted by a group of hunters. One of the party, who had been detailed to stay in the camp as a cook, lazily threw all the supplies into a pot, it is said, and cooked the mixture over a slow fire. When his companions returned, cold and exhausted, they found the concoction a most delicious dish. The time-honored directions for making this luscious meal are: boil about 9 pounds of game—squirrels are preferred—in 2 gallons of water until tender; add to the rich stock 6 pounds of tomatoes, 1 pound of butter-beans, 6 slices of bacon, 1 red pepper, salt to taste; cook 6 hours and add 6 ears of corn cut from the cob; boil for 8 minutes.*
> *Federal Writers' Project, "Part III: Tours," Virginia: A Guide to the Old Dominion*

It's a stew that's easy to personalize with the addition of extra ingredients and spices. Virginians prefer to add both chicken and rabbit to the pot. Georgians add cayenne pepper and prefer a mixture of pork and beef. "Brunswick stew is what happens when small mammals carrying ears of corn fall into barbeque pits," said humorist Roy Blount Jr.

This recipe, featured in the CCC alumni–compiled *Favorite Recipes of the United States Civilian Conservation Corps*, 1933–1942, notes that you'll need "a 50-gallon iron kettle and a good stir paddle" to brew up a proper pot of Brunswick stew. Plan on stirring the pot for four to six hours.

Typically spiked with easily caught critters such as rabbit or squirrel and best prepared in a cauldron over fire, Brunswick stew was a CCC canteen mainstay. *goingtoseedinzone5.com.*

It also calls for a retro ingredient: fatback. Fatback is the slab of hard fat found on both sides of the backbone of a mature pig, usually used for making lard, which means it is not smoked or cured. Pork bacon is the perfect replacement for fatback and can be substituted in a 1:1 ratio.

"The stew is not done until the paddle can stand up in the middle!" declared the Brunswick Stewmasters Association.

Chicken Divan Casserole

Despite its swanky French name—*divan* refers to a meeting place *en français*—Chicken Divan is an all-American chicken casserole. The dish, which is often credited with introducing les Americans to the joys of broccoli, was invented at the Divan Parisien Restaurant in the New York City Chatham Hotel, where it was served as the signature dish in the early twentieth century. Its creator was a chef named Lagasi. No one knows the exact date when the dish was actually created, but it was invented sometime between 1930 and 1940.

Bologna Casserole

As meat prices soared during the Great Depression, people turned to bologna as a cheap source of protein.

Bologna has been produced in its namesake city, Bologna, Italy, since at least the mid-1600s. Italian Americans introduced the finely ground pork sausage containing cubes of pork fat to the United States in the late nineteenth and early twentieth centuries.

But it was a German immigrant who pushed the meatstuff into mainstream America.

Oscar Mayer immigrated to the United States at fourteen years old. His first job was at a meat market in Detroit, Michigan; by 1883, Mayer and his brother Gottfried owned their own meat market in Chicago. Mayer began branding his deli meat treats just in time for the 1893 Chicago World's Fair.

Bologna was fully embraced during the Great Depression, when higher-priced meats were not practical and appeared in sandwiches, casseroles and stews across the United States. This budget-friendly casserole is cheap and filling, the cornerstones of a circa 1930s entrée.

When we would leave camp every morning after breakfast, we would take our mess kits with us because lunch would be served up on the road. A mess kit looks like a frying pan that folds and contains a knife, fork, spoon, and a little cup. At lunchtime, a dump truck would be sent back to camp to pick up the cooks and their "field kitchen." The field kitchen consisted of large containers of whatever food was being served that day. We would line up with our mess kits and pass the mess cans where the cooks would serve our food. We would eat like we worked—hard. After lunch, the cooks would load their field kitchen back in the trunk, and we would go back to work.

—Frank Davis, CCC Company 411

Dark Hollow Falls at Shenandoah National Park, Virginia. Between 1933 and 1942, the CCC built much of the infrastructure of the future Shenandoah National Park in Virginia. "Their achievements included the installation, construction, and landscaping of areas all along Skyline Drive, overlooks, picnic grounds, and developed areas," notes the park's website. *NPS / Shenandoah National Park.*

American Chop Suey

Many legends surround the invention of the dish of stir-fried meat, egg and vegetables known as chop suey.

Culinary anthropologist E.N. Anderson traces the dish to tsap seui (杂碎, "miscellaneous leftovers"), common in China's southern Guangdong province, the home of many early Chinese immigrants to the United States.

Another popular legend is that a Chinese restaurant cook in 1860s San Francisco invented the dish from leftovers to appease rowdy, drunken and hungry miners after hours.

Guangdong-born journalist Liang Qichao wrote in 1903 that a dish known as chop suey had become popular at Chinese restaurants in the United States, though he described the stateside cooking technique as "really awful."

The CCC has done very much for me.

I joined the CCC because I could not secure employment elsewhere and have been in for about three years. I entered the CCC as a cook and still hold the position of a cook.

As long as I have been in the CCC, I have taken advantage of as many opportunities as possible or as time permitted me to. Among the crafts that I have taken, I prefer and have paid more attention to photography and plaster molding. Taking camp shots is my favorite hobby, and as I have learned to develop pictures, it has increased my desire for photography all the more. Plaster molding is very interesting, and I have made many articles in class.

Although I knew how to cook somewhat before I entered the CCC, I did not know what professional field of work I was best qualified for and wanted to do. Since I have been in the CCC, I have found out what work I was best qualified for and will follow after leaving the CCC. This work is cooking, of which I have greatly increased my knowledge and knew I could hold a good position in this work. The CCC not only helped me in cooking, but has taught me how to bake.

The CCC has greatly improved my health and has kept me out of mischief. If it wasn't for the CCC, I might have been a sickly person looking for any odd job, or might have even become desperate in order to get money for food. But thanks to the CCC, it has protected me against all this.

Another important thing the CCC has done is help out my parents a great deal on the allotment money. I think the CCC is the greatest organization ever established for youth, and hope it will forever continue.

—Lee Herron, first cook, CCC Company 1802, Bluffton, Indiana

By the 1920s, the inexpensive dish had become a menu mainstay at luncheonettes across the country.

This recipe, adapted from *Menu and Recipe Suggestions for U.S. C.C.C., Civilian Conservation Corps* by Kellogg's of Battle Creek (1933–1942) creatively recommends serving the dish over buttered Rice Krispies.

1930S BAKED MAC AND CHEESE

Like so many food products, Velveeta Cheese was invented in 1918 by Emil Frey of the Monroe Cheese Company in Monroe, New York, as a means to turn waste into profit. Frey, a Swiss immigrant, melded misshapen Swiss cheese wheels and whey to create the bright orange, "velvety smooth" processed cheese product. In 1927, Frey's firm was purchased by Kraft Foods.

Marketed initially as a nutritious health food, in the 1930s, Velveeta even earned the American Medical Association's seal of approval, citing that its nutritional value built "firm flesh." During the budget-conscious 1930s, Kraft encouraged eating dairy product–based main courses as an economical alternative to more expensive main dishes like meat.

Today, Velveeta incorporates so many additional ingredients and preservatives that it can't legally call itself cheese. Yet it's so ingrained in the American palate that few people can resist a dish of piping hot mac and cheese made with the creamy orange "cheese product."

ZUCCHINI PIE

The premixed biscuit batter known as Bisquick was invented in 1930 by top sales executive Carl Smith. While on a train traveling toward San Francisco, Smith met a clever dining car chef who shared that he pre-mixed lard, flour, baking powder and salt so he could easily bake fresh biscuits quickly on the train every day. Smith worked with food scientists to develop what would be called the "miracle mix." The innovative product appeared on grocery shelves across the United States in 1931 with the tagline "90 seconds from package to oven," and though it was initially

Top: *Sunlight in the Timber* by Edmond J. Fitzgerald. Fitzgerald served with CCC Company 935 at Point Defiance State Park, Tacoma, Washington. This watercolor is now part of the FDR Library and Museum collection. *FDR Presidential Library & Museum.*

Bottom: Ration bag, 1933 USDA Forest Service. "Forest Fire Emergency Ration One Man Day. Stay With Them Till They're Out." "Keep From Freezing, Northern Region Missoula, Montana XXXIII." Natural cotton muslin. Likely used by CCC fire crews. *National Museum of Forest Service History.*

created as a biscuit mix, home cooks soon adapted it for use in recipes for cookies, pancakes, pies, cakes and savory dishes such as this tasty and easy zucchini pie.

SLOPPY JOES

The Sloppy Joes that we know and love today popped up in diners, mess halls and home kitchens in the early twentieth century. Originally known as chopped meat sandwiches or loose meat sandwiches, legend says that they're named after a certain Sioux City, Iowa diner cook named Joe who inventively mixed a can of tomato soup into ground chuck while prepping a loose meat sandwich. Food companies began producing canned Sloppy Joe meat and sauce in the 1960s, but the homemade version is easy to make and tasty, too.

OYSTER STEW

In the landlocked Midwest, oyster stew seems like the unlikeliest holiday tradition of all. Yet oysters have been featured on Christmas Day tables since at least the mid-1800s. Pokagon State Park's CCC Company 556 boasted oyster dressing on its Thanksgiving 1935 holiday menu.

Oysters were plentiful and widely consumed in colonial America. But serving oysters on Christmas Eve began with Irish immigrants, who substituted the dried ling fish traditionally served in their homeland with oysters.

Left: Group of CCC boys from Idaho just arrived in camp near Andersonville, Tennessee, October 1933. The CCC units were to assist in the reforestation work on the Clinch River watershed above the dam. *The U.S. National Archives, Flickr.*

Opposite: CCC at an experimental farm in Beltsville, Maryland. *FDR Presidential Library & Museum.*

Petrified Forest National Park's rustic Painted Desert Inn's main building and associated guest cabins (casitas) were designed in the Pueblo Revival style by National Park Service architect Lyle E. Bennett and others from the Park Service Branch of Plans and Design. Construction was carried out by CCC builders and artisans from 1937 to 1940. "When you visit Petrified Forest National Park and drive the roads, hike a trail, or explore the Painted Desert Inn, take a few moments to reflect on the CCC, the men who labored on these projects, and the investment America made during its most desperate economic period," notes the park's website. *Cscccl, Wikimedia Commons.*

Top: Painted Desert Inn, Petrified Forest National Park, Arizona. *SCA_ Chimera, Flickr*.

Bottom: Painted Desert Inn, Petrified Forest National Park, Arizona. *Petrified Forest.NPS, Flickr*.

Thanks to the fact that they can easily stay fresh due to their naturally protective shells, oysters reached the Midwest packed in ice via trains by the mid-1800s. Since the trip from the coast to the Midwest took days via rail, fresh oysters were typically consumed in cooler months, when the chilly temperatures kept them safe for consumption despite the long journey. Oysters were cheap, too: in the early 1900s, a pound of fresh oysters cost half as much as a pound of beef.

Springfield, Illinois–based food writer Peter Glatz shared this recipe with the *Illinois Times*, noting, "This easy recipe is full of rich, wonderful seafood flavor. A family tradition, I've been enjoying this stew each Christmas Eve for as long as I can remember."

Civilian Conservation Corps Vegetable Soup

1 medium onion, finely diced

3 tablespoons butter

2 cups diced potatoes

2 cups diced celery

2 cups diced carrots

2 cups of frozen peas

1 (13-ounce) package summer sausage or ring bologna, sliced and halved (we also like to use Polish sausage)

12 cups water

½ cup milk

5 tablespoons flour

Salt and pepper to taste

In a skillet over medium heat, sauté the onions in butter until translucent. Add the celery and stir for one minute. Add the other veggies and meat and stir for one minute. Add the water and bring to a boil; then turn down the heat just enough to keep a steady simmer. Simmer until the veggies are tender, about one hour.

In a small bowl, whisk flour and milk until it forms a smooth paste. Slowly stir the mixture into the simmering soup until the soup thickens. Season with salt and pepper and serve hot.

Navy Bean Soup

1 cup dried white beans

8 cups water

1 ham bone

1 onion, minced

2 tablespoons butter

¼ cup celery leaves, chopped

2 tablespoons flour

Salt and pepper to taste

Rinse the navy beans with hot water. Soak in warm water for about 4 hours or, better, overnight.

Drain the beans and put them in a large pot with 8 cups of water and the ham hock. Simmer on low heat for about 2 hours or until the beans are soft.

Brown the minced onion in butter, stir in the celery leaves, followed by the flour, then add the mixture to the soup. Simmer on low heat for 30 more minutes. Add salt and pepper to taste before serving.

Chipped Beef on Toast

4 tablespoons butter, melted
4 tablespoons flour, sifted
1 cup evaporated milk
1 cup beef stock
1 cup dried or chipped beef, chopped
Cayenne pepper
Sprig parsley, finely chopped
Toasted bread

Mix melted fat and flour; still until smooth. Mix evaporated milk and beef stock over medium heat. Gradually add fat and flour mixture, stirring constantly. Add chipped beef and pepper. Reduce heat and simmer for about ten minutes. Garnish with parsley and serve hot over toast.

Bread and Butter Pickles

6 cups pickling cucumbers, thinly sliced

2 tablespoons kosher salt

1 cup thinly sliced sweet onion

1 cup sugar

1½ cups vinegar

¼ cup packed light brown sugar

2 teaspoons mustard seeds

1 teaspoon celery seeds

Mix the cucumbers with salt in a bowl; cover and chill for 2 hours.

Rinse the cucumbers in a colander under cold water. Place rinsed cucumbers in a bowl and mix in the onions.

In a saucepan, stir the sugar and the remaining ingredients over medium heat and whisk until the sugar dissolves. Pour the hot vinegar mixture over the cucumber and onion mixture. Cover and refrigerate 24 hours.

Store the pickles in an airtight container in the refrigerator for up to 2 weeks.

Have you ever gone to the highest point around and looked at the gigantic panorama spread out below? Hills, valleys, streams, perhaps a waterfall, trees, and the sky. Nature, the master painter, is there at her best. A beautiful design, that man for all his creative genius cannot approach. A picture that the greatest artist finds it hard to reproduce because the very spirit of the picture is so hard to define. These things, and, in fact, nature in all its phases is the handiwork of God, but man must have been the prized creation of all, to be given a power and understanding with which to love and enjoy these things, even as God himself must love and enjoy them.

—Enrollee Charles W. Massie, Company 513, Henryville, Indiana

Brunswick Stew

2 pounds cooked and diced boneless, skinless chicken (can also substitute rabbit, squirrel or pork)

6–7 slices of bacon, cooked and chopped

3 cups diced potatoes

1 cup cooked and mashed sweet potatoes

3 cups corn

1 medium onion, chopped

1½ cups tomato sauce

1 teaspoon cayenne pepper

3 tablespoons Worcestershire sauce

Salt to taste

Place all ingredients in a stockpot or Dutch oven and bring to a boil. Reduce the heat to low and cover the pan; simmer until hot and bubbly, about 1 hour.

Chicken Divan Casserole

1½ pounds of fresh broccoli cut into bite-sized pieces

1½ cups shredded Cheddar cheese

½ cup milk

2 (10-ounce) cans cream of chicken soup

¾ cup sour cream

1 teaspoon garlic powder

½ teaspoon dry mustard

Salt and pepper to taste

3 cups cooked chicken breasts, cubed

Topping

3 tablespoons melted butter

1 cup butter crackers, crumbled

Preheat the oven to 400°F. Place broccoli in a large pot of boiling water and cook for about 3 minutes, until slightly tender. Drain.

Combine 1 cup Cheddar cheese, milk, condensed soup, sour cream and seasonings in a bowl. Stir in broccoli and chicken and pour into a casserole dish. Sprinkle with remaining cheese.

In a bowl, mix the butter and cracker crumbs. Sprinkle the topping over the chicken mixture. Bake for 20 minutes, or until the breadcrumbs are golden.

Bologna Casserole

6 slices of bacon, chopped
1 onion, diced
1 pound all-beef bologna, cubed
1 (15-ounce) can baked beans
1 (15-ounce) can chili beans with sauce, undrained
1 jar pimentos, drained
2 cups shredded Cheddar cheese

Preheat the oven to 350 degrees. In a small skillet over medium-high heat, brown the bacon and onion.

Stir the cubed bologna, beans, chili beans, pimentos, bacon and onions in a greased baking dish. Top with the shredded Cheddar cheese.

Bake for 20 minutes or until the mixture is bubbly and the cheese is golden.

Cabbage Soup

3 tablespoons butter
4 cups chopped green cabbage
4 large carrots, peeled and chopped
3 ribs celery, finely chopped
1 medium onion, finely chopped
4 cups chicken or vegetable broth
1 small (14-ounce) can diced tomatoes
1 teaspoon salt
¼ teaspoon pepper

In a large soup pot, heat butter over medium heat. Add cabbage, carrots, celery and onion and cook, stirring often, until onion is translucent, about 5 minutes.

Add broth, tomatoes, salt and pepper. Bring to a simmer, cover and reduce heat to medium-low. Simmer, stirring occasionally, until all vegetables are tender (40–60 minutes, depending on your preferred consistency).

Season with salt and pepper to taste and serve.

Cabbage soup, cheap and satisfying. *Wikimedia Commons / Silar.*

Rice Tomato Soup

This simple soup can easily be prepared in a pot over an open fire. Adapted from the U.S. Department of Agriculture Forest Service's 1928 Fire Camp Cookbook.

3 (84-ounce) cans crushed tomatoes
9 cups chicken broth (or 9 chicken bouillon cubes plus 9 cups of water)
1½ cups rice
1 cup macaroni
Salt and pepper to taste

Place the tomatoes and broth in an open-fire cooking pot. Boil slowly for about five minutes. Add the rice and macaroni to the boiling water and cook for about ten minutes or until done. Season with salt and pepper to taste.

Six-Layer Casserole

2 cups ground beef
Salt and pepper to taste
1 tablespoon garlic powder
2 cups thinly sliced potatoes
2 cups chopped celery
2 cups kidney beans (canned)
2 cups diced onion
2 cups diced green peppers
1½ cups ketchup

Preheat the oven to 375 degrees. In a skillet over medium heat, brown ground beef and flavor with salt, pepper and garlic powder.

In a 9x13-inch casserole pan, layer potatoes, celery, kidney beans, onion and green peppers. Top with ground beef, and cover with ketchup. Cover the pan with aluminum foil and bake for 1½ hours.

Spinach Baked with Corn Flakes

Spinach and...corn flakes? Though the combination sounds suspect, this dinner dish is a tasty way to serve vitamin and fiber-rich spinach. Recipe adapted from Menu and Recipe Suggestions for U.S. C.C.C., Civilian Conservation Corps, *Kellogg's of Battle Creek, 1933–1942.*

1 small onion, chopped

1 medium green pepper, chopped

1 tablespoon plus ¼ cup butter

3 cups spinach

⅔ cup corn flakes

Salt and pepper to taste

Sauté chopped onion and green pepper in a tablespoon of butter until tender. Mix in spinach. Place in a shallow casserole or baking dish. Top with corn flakes. Drizzle ¼ cup of melted butter on top of the corn flakes.

Bake at 400 degrees until the corn flakes are golden brown, about 20 minutes.

Corn Oysters

3 cups corn, cut from the cob or canned

6 egg yolks

Salt and pepper to taste

6 egg whites, beaten until stiff

Mix the corn, slightly beaten egg yolks and seasonings. Fold in stiffly beaten egg whites. Drop by spoonfuls onto a greased griddle and pan fry until golden. Serve hot.

Recipe adapted from Menu and Recipe Suggestions for U.S. C.C.C., Civilian Conservation Corps, *Kellogg's of Battle Creek, 1933–1942.*

Venison Stew

This stew requires a campfire and likely would have been prepared at CCC spike side camps consisting of ten to twenty men living in tents near work sites located deep within the forest. This recipe for venison stew is featured in Camp Cooking *by the National Museum of Forest Service History.*

½ cup flour

1 teaspoon onion powder

1 teaspoon garlic powder

1 teaspoon seasoned salt

1 teaspoon crushed sage

2 pounds venison or elk, cut into cubes

2 tablespoons vegetable oil

1 pound carrots, cut into ½-inch chunks

5 large Idaho russet potatoes, cut into cubes

1 medium onion, cut into chunks

Salt and pepper to taste

Put the flour and the seasoning in a bowl and mix together. Dredge the meat in the mixture.

Brown the meat in vegetable oil in a 12-inch Dutch oven, and then add the veggies. Cover the mixture with water to the top of the ingredients.

Cook with 8 briquettes on the bottom and 15 briquettes on top until the spuds and carrots are tender to a fork, about 45 minutes.

To thicken the broth, add some of the flour mixture to your liking. Salt and pepper to taste.

Salmon Salad

2 (5-ounce) cans of red salmon
½ cup celery, chopped
1 tablespoon capers
1 cup Kellogg's Corn Flakes
Juice of one lemon
½ cup mayonnaise

Combine all the ingredients and lightly toss together until well mixed. Arrange on crisp lettuce or watercress.

Recipe adapted from *Menu and Recipe Suggestions for U.S. C.C.C., Civilian Conservation Corps*, Kellogg's of Battle Creek, 1933–1942.

American Chop Suey

2 onions, diced
2 tablespoons canola oil
½ pound pork, cubed
1 green pepper, diced
½ cup sliced mushrooms
1 cup chopped celery
¼ cup rice (uncooked)
3 cups chicken stock
Salt and pepper to taste

Sauté onions in oil; add pork and cook until seared. Add remaining ingredients. Cook slowly over medium heat until vegetables, meat and rice are tender, about 20 minutes. Pour over buttered Rice Krispies and serve.

Three-Pound Meatloaf

This recipe by John R. Graves, a former CCC mess sergeant from Fall Creek Falls, Virginia, was featured in the tome Favorite Recipes of the CCC Alumni. *Graves notes, "It is a three-pound meatloaf with the anticipation that some will be leftover—because there is nothing better than cold meatloaf sandwiches with a dash of catsup."*

2 pounds ground beef

1 pound spicy pork sausage

1 egg

1 cup breadcrumbs (or cracker crumbs, oatmeal, cornflakes or even wheatgerm)

1 cup finely chopped onions

1 tablespoon dry mustard

2 tablespoons Worcestershire sauce

1 (8-ounce) can tomato sauce

2 cloves garlic, finely chopped

3 tablespoons tomato paste

Optional: 3 tablespoons green pepper, finely chopped

Preheat the oven to 400 degrees.

Now it is time to mix thoroughly with your hands (then you wash your hands only once afterward). I mean mix well. If you care to taste, put a small dab in the skillet for a minute and taste it—I have done it without frying it.

Blend all the ingredients save for the tomato paste and form into a square loaf, about 2 inches thick (bread loaf pans are OK, but I like the thinner loaf better). If it is too big, freeze half for a later bake. Shape into a Pyrex loaf pan, covering loosely with foil. Turn the oven back to about 230 degrees and bake on the middle rack. After about 45 minutes, remove the foil, pour off juice and fat (save for soup stock), spread tomato paste over the meatloaf and bake at about 275 degrees for another half hour, or until the top is slightly brown.

Let set a few minutes before slicing. The next day you will savor a great cold meatloaf sandwich. Serves 3 chowhounds or 6 normal people.

Note: Make sure the oven is preheated to 400 degrees and lowered to 250 degrees; raise the temperature again when the oven is open to pour off fat and juice.

Snowflake Potatoes

Snowflake mashed potatoes were a regular option on menus at nicer hotels, trains, ships and restaurants until the 1950s. They also appeared on CCC holiday menus.

4 pounds potatoes, boiled and mashed
1 (8-ounce) package cream cheese, softened
1 cup sour cream
2 tablespoons salt
1 tablespoon pepper
2 cloves garlic, minced
½ cup chopped chives
3 tablespoons butter, melted
½ teaspoon paprika

Mix potatoes, cheese, sour cream, salt, pepper and garlic. Stir in chives. Set the mixture in a greased baking pan.

Pour melted butter on top and sprinkle with paprika. Bake at 350 degrees for about 40 minutes or until golden.

Fancy Olives

Stuffed olives appeared on several CCC holiday menus. From the late 1800s until the 1960s, olives were a must on holiday tables.

1 (8-ounce) jar pitted jumbo green olives
1 (9-ounce) package cream cheese, softened
¼ pound thin sliced corned beef lunchmeat, finely minced
1 teaspoon garlic powder
Salt and pepper to taste
Toothpicks

Dry the olives with paper towels. Cut a slit from the top to the bottom of each olive. Set aside.

Combine cream cheese, minced corned beef lunchmeat, garlic powder, salt and pepper in a mixing bowl. Mix well.

Fill a plastic bag with the cream cheese mixture. Cut a small hole in one corner of the plastic bag and pipe the cream cheese mixture into jumbo olives.

Chill before serving with toothpicks.

Ham and Celery Loaf

Like olives, celery in some form was a must-have on holiday tables. This recipe is adapted from one featured in the April 19, 1931 edition of the Indianapolis Star.

1 package lime Jell-O
1¾ cups boiling water
¼ cup vinegar
½ teaspoon salt
1 cup cooked ham, finely chopped
1½ cups celery, finely chopped
1 tablespoon grated onion
3 sweet pickles, finely chopped
Optional: fresh watercress for garnish

Dissolve Jell-O in boiling water. Stir in vinegar and salt. When slightly thickened, fold in the ham, celery, onion and pickles. Pour into a loaf pan. Chill until firm.

Unmold and serve in slices garnished with fresh watercress.

Pittsburgh Potatoes

4 cups cubed potatoes

1 medium onion, minced

3 tablespoons pimientos, chopped

1 can cream of chicken soup

1 cup sour cream

2 cups corn flakes (or bread crumbs)

4 tablespoons butter, melted

Salt and pepper to taste

1½ cups shredded Cheddar cheese

Cook the potato cubes and onion together in salted, boiling water for five minutes. Drain and place in a buttered casserole pan.

Mix the pimientos, soup and sour cream in a separate bowl. Pour over the potatoes.

Sprinkle the corn flakes on top, and then drizzle with the butter. Sprinkle with Cheddar cheese and salt and pepper to taste.

Bake at 350 degrees for 45 minutes, or until the corn flake topping is golden.

I remember being hungry for lots of days....The Depression hit and everybody lost everything. Healthy family men would commit suicide just about every day. And I never understood that until I got older, and it stayed with me all the years. I got hungry and I didn't have a job. No education, only up to the 6th grade and so I applied as a volunteer in 1940. They sent us from Atlanta to Oregon...and it was hard work, rain or shine you went. We had some of the hardest foremen, but they always listened....They would always encourage you to push a little more. Learn a little bit.

—John West, enrollee, CCC Camp Klamel, Murrell, Oregon

Peanut Butter, Bacon and Chili Sauce Sandwiches

The creamy peanut butter we know and love today was introduced in 1932 when Skippy Peanut Butter, named (without copyright permission) after the popular Skippy comic strip (1923–1945), was introduced by Alameda, California food packer Joseph L. Rosefield. The CCC enrollees enjoyed peanut butter sandwiches, but savory combinations were preferred over today's classic jelly pairing. In addition to this recipe for peanut butter, bacon and chili sauce sandwiches, the official CCC mess hall recipes also includes instructions for peanut butter, onion and mayonnaise sandwiches.

Bacon, cooked (2 slices per sandwich)
Peanut butter (about ¼ cup per sandwich)
Chili sauce (1 tablespoon per sandwich)

In a small bowl, mix the peanut butter and chili sauce. Spread between slices of bread and top with two slices of bacon.

1930s Baked Mac and Cheese

8 ounces elbow macaroni
2½ cups milk
8 tablespoons butter
¼ cup flour
¼ teaspoon Worcestershire sauce
⅛ teaspoon ground red pepper
1 (8-ounce) package of Velveeta
⅔ cup crushed Ritz crackers

Preheat the oven to 375 degrees. Cook the elbow macaroni according to package instructions until al dente. Drain and set aside.

Scald the milk: heat in a heavy bottomed saucepan over medium heat, stirring frequently until small bubbles appear around the outside of the saucepan, or the temperature registers 180 to 185 degrees.

In a large saucepan over medium heat, melt 4 tablespoons of the butter. Stir in the flour until smooth. Whisk in milk and continue whisking until the mixture comes to a boil. Whisk for 1 minute more, until the sauce is thickened. Remove from heat and stir in Worcestershire sauce and red pepper. Stir in cheese until melted. Stir in cooked, drained macaroni. Spoon into a well-greased casserole.

In a small saucepan, melt the remaining 2 tablespoons of butter. Remove from heat and stir in the crushed Ritz crackers. Sprinkle the cracker crumbs over the macaroni.

Bake for 25 to 30 minutes, or until the sauce is bubbly and the cracker crumbs are golden brown.

Porcupine Meatballs

Porcupine meatballs were a Depression-era favorite because they stretched a pound of ground beef into a hearty, tasty dish that could feed a crew. Once the secret budget-stretching ingredient—rice—is cooked, it sticks out of the meatballs like porcupine quills.

1 pound ground beef

¼ cup long grain rice

1 egg, slightly beaten

¼ cup onion, minced

1 teaspoon garlic powder

1 teaspoon paprika

1 teaspoon pepper

1 teaspoon salt

1 (10.75-ounce) can condensed tomato soup

½ cup water

3 teaspoons Worcestershire sauce

In a mixing bowl, combine meat, rice, egg, onion, garlic powder, paprika, pepper, salt and ¼ cup of the canned condensed tomato soup. Shape into about 20 meatballs and place in a greased skillet.

Mix remaining soup, water and Worcestershire sauce. Pour over the meatballs in the skillet. Bring to a boil and reduce heat. Cover and simmer for about 40 minutes or until the meatballs are cooked thoroughly, stirring often.

Mexican Spaghetti

This Mexican take on classic Italian spaghetti with red sauce is truly a one-pot wonder.

1 pound ground beef
1 medium yellow onion, diced
1 (7-ounce) can diced green chilies, undrained
1 (14.5-ounce) can diced tomatoes, undrained
1 cup frozen corn, thawed and drained
1 (8-ounce) can tomato sauce
2 cups water
8 ounces dried spaghetti, broken in thirds
1 cup grated Cheddar cheese

In a large skillet over medium heat, brown beef and onion until the beef is thoroughly cooked. Drain fat.

Stir in green chilies, diced tomatoes, corn, tomato sauce and water, and bring to a boil. Stir in spaghetti. Reduce the heat and simmer, covered, for 20 minutes or until the pasta is al dente.

Sprinkle individual plates of Mexican spaghetti with cheddar cheese.

Zucchini Pie

2 medium zucchini, grated (about 3 cups)

1 small onion, minced

1 cup Bisquick

⅓ cup vegetable oil

½ cup grated cheese

4 eggs

In a bowl, mix the zucchini, onion, Bisquick, vegetable oil and cheese. Beat eggs lightly and stir well into the other ingredients.

Pour into a greased 10-inch pie dish and bake at 350 degrees for 30 minutes, or until golden.

Sloppy Joes

1 pound ground chuck

½ cup condensed tomato soup

½ cup ketchup

1 tablespoon mustard

1 tablespoon brown sugar

1 tablespoon apple cider vinegar

1 teaspoon salt

1 teaspoon onion powder

½ teaspoon celery seed

In a large skillet, fully cook the beef over medium heat. Drain. Stir in the soup, ketchup, mustard, brown sugar, vinegar, salt, onion powder and celery seed and bring to a boil. Reduce heat, then simmer uncovered for 10 minutes. Serve on fresh buns.

Asparagus Casserole

Adapted from a recipe by Athleen M. Adams of Richmond, Virginia, CCC Pocahontas Chapter 124, featured in Favorite Recipes of the CCC Alumni. *Two cups of fresh chopped asparagus can be substituted for the canned asparagus.*

1½ cups saltine cracker crumbs

½ cup chopped almonds, toasted

¾ stick butter

1 tablespoon Worcestershire sauce

1 can cream of mushroom soup

¾ cup shredded Cheddar cheese

2 (15-ounce) cans of chopped asparagus (save the liquid from the cans)

In a small bowl, mix together the cracker crumbs and chopped almonds; set aside.

In a medium-sized saucepan over medium heat, combine the butter, Worcestershire sauce, mushroom soup, cheese and the liquid from the asparagus cans and heat until blended.

Set the asparagus in a greased casserole dish. Top with half of the sauce. Top with half of the crumb mixture. Repeat. Bake for 30 minutes at 350 degrees, or until the crumbs are golden.

I gained about 20 pounds…the food was good! At first I was part of the Kitchen Police. There were about 350 men there.…Can you imagine washing all those dishes and silverware for all those people three times a day! We'd get up at about 5:00 a.m. and get up about 8:00 a.m. But we had good food! I had cold cuts on Sunday nights and hotcakes on Sunday mornings.

—Forrest Fields, enrollee at the CCC Camp at Fort Pulaski, Georgia, 1938-1940

Stuffed Peppers

6 medium bell peppers

½ pound ground beef, cooked

½ pound cooked ham

3 tablespoons chopped onion

2 cups Kellogg's Rice Krispies cereal

1 teaspoon salt

1 teaspoon pepper

1¼ cups tomato juice (can also substitute tomato sauce)

Remove and discard the bell peppers' tops, seeds and membranes. Wash. Parboil for about 5 minutes in boiling salted water. Drain.

In a mixing bowl, combine meats, onion and Rice Krispies. Add seasonings and tomato juice, stirring to combine.

Fill green peppers with meat mixture and arrange upright in muffin-pan cups coated with cooking spray.

Bake at 350 degrees for about 30 minutes or until peppers are tender and done. Serve hot.

Calico Beans

¼ pound bacon, diced

1 pound ground beef

1 (15-ounce) can pork and beans

1 (15-ounce) can kidney beans

1 (15-ounce) can lima beans

½ cup chopped onion

½ cup brown sugar

½ cup ketchup

1 teaspoon dried mustard

1 teaspoon salt

2 teaspoons apple cider vinegar

In a large skillet, cook the bacon until crispy. Set aside the bacon and place the ground beef and onion in the same skillet and cook beef thoroughly. Drain the fat.

Mix the beef, onions, beans, brown sugar, ketchup, dried mustard and apple cider vinegar and pour into a greased 13x9-inch (or similar size) ovenproof pan. Top with bacon, then bake until beans are bubbly and sauce is the consistency of pancake syrup, about 2 hours. Let stand to thicken slightly and serve.

Oyster Stew

1 pint fresh raw oysters, with their liquor
1 quart whole milk
4 tablespoons unsalted butter
1 shallot, minced
1 small garlic clove, minced
2 tablespoons all-purpose flour
1 cup half-and-half
2 tablespoons sherry
½ teaspoon Worcestershire sauce
⅛ teaspoon celery salt
Kosher salt, to taste
Freshly ground black pepper, to taste
Fresh lemon juice, to taste
A few dashes of hot sauce (such as Tabasco or Frank's Redhot)
Minced fresh parsley

Place the oysters in a colander with a slotted spoon, reserving the liquor. Rinse the oysters well under cold water. Remove oysters to a bowl and set them aside. Line the colander with a layer of cheesecloth, and with a bowl underneath, strain the oyster liquor to remove any grit.

In a saucepan, heat the milk and reserved oyster liquor just to the boiling point, but do not allow it to boil. Whisk constantly to prevent scorching until the mixture just begins to steam, about 3 to 4 minutes. Add the oysters and poach for about 4 to 5 minutes or until the edges of the oysters just begin to curl. Remove the pan from heat. Transfer oysters to a plate with a slotted spoon to prevent overcooking.

Melt the butter in a large saucepan over medium heat. Add the shallot and garlic and cook, stirring often, 4 minutes or until tender. Sprinkle flour over shallots and garlic and cook, constantly whisking, until completely incorporated and bubbly, about 3 to 4 minutes. Gradually whisk in the half-and-half, sherry, Worcestershire sauce and celery salt.

Bring to a boil and add the milk mixture, stirring constantly. Reduce heat to medium-low and add the oysters. Cook until just warmed through. Season to taste with salt, pepper, lemon juice and hot sauce.

Transfer oysters into four individual bowls with a slotted spoon and ladle over the broth to serve. Sprinkle with additional pepper. Garnish with parsley leaves. Serve with oyster crackers on the side. Note: Fresh oysters are preferable, but canned or jarred oysters can be used when fresh raw oysters are unavailable.

There were three cooks per shift, and two shifts, so a total of six cooks and one baker. On Christmas, we all pitched in, even our mess sergeant. We started the feast with oyster stew. Now that was a rare delicacy for the Depression era, and for the Northwoods. We had roast goose with oyster and sage dressing, mashed white potatoes, and baked sweet potatoes with brown pan gravy. There was also fresh lettuce salad, celery sticks, olives, raisin bread, sweet and sour pickles, cranberry relish, mincemeat pie, cookies, nuts, and candies. I know there were lots of folks who weren't eating all that well on Christmas day, 1934. Eating at our camp that day were three lieutenants, an educational advisor, a superintendent, a head foreman, a surveyor, a mechanic, 13 leaders, 21 assistant leaders, and 224 enrollees. That's a lot of oyster stew.

—Guy Christianson, enrollee at Camp Connors Lake, Phillips, Wisconsin

Devils Tower National Monument, Wyoming. CCC crews stationed at Wyoming's striking Devils Tower National Monument from 1935 to the early 1940s constructed park roads, trails and the ponderosa pine log building that once served as the main visitor center. *NPS / Devils Tower National Monument.*

Spaghetti with Bacon

8 ounces uncooked spaghetti

½ pound bacon strips, chopped

1 medium onion, chopped

1 (14½-ounce) can diced tomatoes, undrained

1 (8-ounce) can tomato sauce

Preheat the oven to 350 degrees. Cook the spaghetti for half the time as instructed on the package. (It should be al dente.) Drain and transfer to a greased 11x7-inch baking dish.

In a skillet over medium heat, cook the bacon and onion until the bacon is crispy. Drain fat. Stir in tomatoes and tomato sauce.

Spread sauce on top of the spaghetti and bake, covered with aluminum foil, until bubbly, about 35 minutes.

LARGE-BATCH
SUPPER RECIPES

Brunswick Stew for One Hundred

75 pounds of small game (chicken, rabbit, squirrel)

15 gallons water

25 pounds of beef with bone

2 pounds fatback

100 pounds of potatoes, cut into ½- to ¾-inch pieces

20 pounds onions, chopped

30 quarts tomatoes, chopped

32 quarts butter beans

10 pounds of sweet potatoes, cooked and mashed, used to thicken the stew

2 gallons tomato sauce

3 pounds butter

32 quarts shoepeg corn

Place all the meat and fatback in a massive pot filled with water and cook until done. Remove all meat and bone from the pot. Separate meat from bones and skin. Return de-boned and de-skinned meat to the pot.

Add potatoes, onions, tomatoes and butterbeans to the pot. Cook over medium heat, stirring often, for about 4½ hours, until the soup begins to thicken.

Add the mashed sweet potatoes, tomato sauce and butter; cook about ½ hour more. Add the corn. Turn off the flame but continue to stir the pot often until the stew cools down to a reasonable, warm serving temperature.

Chipped Beef on Toast for One Hundred

7 pounds dried or chipped beef
4½ cups butter, melted
2¼ cups flour, sifted
4 (14½-ounce) cans evaporated milk
4 gallons beef stock
2 bunches parsley, finely chopped
1 tablespoon black (or cayenne) pepper
130 slices of bread (about 12 pounds), toasted

Separate the chipped beef into small pieces. Mix melted fat and flour; still until smooth.

Mix evaporated milk and beef stock over medium heat. Gradually add fat and flour mixture, stirring constantly. Add chipped beef and pepper. Reduce heat and simmer for about ten minutes. Serve hot over toast.

Irish Stew for One Hundred

Best cooked in a kettle over an open fire, Irish stew is one of Ireland's most famous traditional dishes.

25 pounds of beef suitable for stewing (from less tender cuts) or leftover beef, diced into ½-inch cubes
4 pounds onions, chopped
2 quarts beef stock
25 pounds potatoes, peeled and diced
1 pound flour
Salt and pepper to taste

Brown beef and onions. Add the beef stock and potatoes and simmer for three hours. Whisk in the flour and simmer for one more hour. Season with salt and pepper to taste before serving.

Baked Beans for One Hundred

This classic American recipe was included in the Thirty Day Menus and Tested Special Recipes for CCC Companies *with the note: "This recipe was obtained from the U.S. Naval Academy, Annapolis, Maryland."*

15 pounds white navy beans
4 cups molasses
8 tablespoons sugar
5 teaspoons Worcestershire sauce
3 tablespoons dry mustard
5 tablespoons salt
4 pounds bacon

Soak beans overnight in cold water. In the morning, drain, recover with water, bring to boiling point and simmer until tender.

Drain the beans and return to a greased roasting pan. Stir in molasses, sugar, Worcestershire sauce, salt and mustard.

Heat oil over high heat and add bacon and cook for 2–3 minutes until the fat has rendered off. (Keep the fat, as it will add flavor to the baked beans). Mix the bacon (and fat) into the beans with a long-handled wooden spoon.

Cover the beans with water.

Bake covered for 3–4 hours in a 300-degree oven. Stir every hour, replenishing water when necessary so the beans don't dry out. Uncover for the last hour of baking to brown the beans.

―❧―

Pork Roast for One Hundred Men

50 pounds pork (loin, shoulder or butt)
Salt and pepper to taste
2 sticks (16 tablespoons) butter

Cut the pork into pieces weighing about 5 pounds each; wipe with a damp cloth. Rub generously with salt and pepper.

Place the butter in a roasting pan on top of the stove and sear the meat until all sides are well browned.

Place the roasts in an uncovered roasting pan in a 325-degree oven until well done (30 minutes per pound).

Baked Bean Salad for One Hundred

8 pounds baked beans
2 pounds onion, minced
2 pounds sweet pickles, chopped fine
3 tablespoons mustard
1½ cups mayonnaise
1½ cups vinegar
2 heads lettuce
Salt and pepper to taste

Mix all ingredients thoroughly and season to taste with salt, pepper, mustard and vinegar. Serve cold. Serve each portion on one lettuce leaf.

Potato Salad for One Hundred

25 pounds potatoes, boiled and diced
5 pounds celery, diced
2 pounds bacon, diced and browned
1½ cups vinegar
5 cups mayonnaise
Salt and pepper to taste

Mix the diced potatoes, celery and the chopped onions.
Fry the bacon until brown and while still hot, pour over the veggie mixture.
Add the vinegar and mayonnaise and mix well.
Season with salt and pepper to taste. Serve chilled.

Oxtail Soup for One Hundred

8 pounds beef tails, chopped into 1-inch cubes
4 pounds carrots, diced
4 pounds onions, diced
2 cups olive oil
7 gallons beef stock
4 (14-ounce) cans crushed tomatoes
2 tablespoons celery salt
Salt and pepper to taste
1 pound flour
8 sticks (4 cups) butter

Spread beef tails on a shallow roasting pan. Roast at 450 degrees F (230 degrees C) for 45 minutes.

In a large stock pot, sauté onion and carrots in olive oil. Add browned oxtails. Add beef stock, tomatoes and celery salt. Bring to boil, and then reduce heat. Cover, and simmer slowly for 2 hours.

Brown the flour in the butter over medium heat, stirring constantly. Stir in 2 cups of the beef broth and mix until well combined. Add to the oxtails/broth. Salt and pepper to taste before serving.

Lima Beans for One Hundred

15 pounds dried lima beans
2 pounds of bacon, sliced; ham hocks; or salt pork
Salt and pepper to taste

Rinse the beans in cold water. Soak the beans in cold water: In colder months, soak overnight or 8 hours, but in hotter months, the beans may sour if soaked this long, so soak for 2 hours.

After soaking the beans, drain and place in a large pot. Add the sliced bacon and enough fresh water to cover. Season to taste with salt and pepper and simmer until tender, about 2 to 5 hours, depending on how long the beans were soaked. Serve hot.

Bread Rolls for One Hundred

2 pounds sugar
4 tablespoons salt
8 sticks (4 cups) butter
1 tablespoon ground mace (or nutmeg)
1 tablespoon lemon extract
15 eggs
2 cups dry active yeast
17 pounds flour
1 gallon milk
2 cups of butter, melted

Preheat the oven to 350 degrees. Cream thoroughly the sugar, salt, butter, mace and lemon extract; then add eggs gradually and cream until light. Dissolve the yeast in ¼ of the liquid, which should be at a temperature of about 80 degrees.

Add the yeast to the creamed ingredients, then gradually mix in the flour and milk. Mix until the dough is smooth and free from lumps and form into about five large balls.

Cover the dough balls with a dish towel and let rise. If the temperature is 80 degrees or higher, allow about 45 minutes to rise; in cold weather, allow about 1 hour.

Gently punch the dough down and form into bun-sized balls. Cover again with a dish towel and let rise for an additional 20 minutes.

Place the buns on a greased baking sheet. Bake for about 20 minutes or until golden brown. Brush with melted butter before serving.

The canteen was a neat long building housing tables, complete with pen and paper for writing home, and some books and newspapers donated by nearby town people. There were the usual candy and cigarettes for sale, as well as shaving supplies. There was always some 3.2 beer (low alcoholic), soda pop, and snacks available. We had a ping-pong table, and that was the scene of many an all-night game between some of the guys, who were betting on the outcome.

The mess hall was a long building with two rows of tables lining the sidewalls. We usually kept the tables set up for the next meal. There were three potbellied barrel stoves, all shined up with stove black to keep us warm. The winter of 1934 was a pretty cold winter, as I recall. There was a fireman who worked all night keeping up all the fires. Those stoves needed filling about every two hours. There were ceiling lights hanging down from the middle of the room, with black cone-shaped shades. There was a piano at one end of the mess hall, and we had a lot of sing-alongs. We had the best piano player you ever heard, a guy by the name of Steen from Eau Claire, Wisconsin. When Steen first signed on, he was a potato peeler. He could out-peel every guy in camp with those fingers. He could play beautiful classical music as well as popular tunes. We started a barbershop quartet and ended up with a pretty good glee club.

—Guy Christianson, enrollee at Camp Connors Lake, Phillips, Wisconsin

DESSERTS AND HOLIDAYS

CCC camps served a dessert with every evening meal, a big deal for the enrollees, many of whom entered the camps underweight. CCC menus feature countless delectable desserts: cakes, cookies galore and every type of pie under the sun.

Holidays were also celebrated in the CCC mess hall. The CCC camps served as a home away from home for enrollees, many of whom traveled far to work on CCC projects, the majority of which were situated in the western states. The kitchen staff worked hard to prepare Thanksgiving and Christmas menus, and the enrollees decorated the mess hall, adding extra delight and a sense of home to the holiday season. Other holidays were celebrated, too: one example is the CCC Rosh Hashanah observance hosted by Rabbi Julius Leibert, together with Catholic and Protestant chaplains, in Spokane, Washington, in 1935. It was attended by over two hundred Jewish CCC members, most of whom were originally from Brooklyn, the Bronx and Trenton, New Jersey.

CCC Company 556's Thanksgiving menu from 1935 reflects a typical, bountiful holiday meal.

MOCK APPLE PIE

An apple pie minus the apples? Sounds crazy, right?

Then again, apples aren't always in season. And crackers are cheaper than apples.

What's a Depression-era cook to do?

Creatively substitute crackers for apples, of course!

The result tastes surprisingly like apples. The pie looks like apple pie, and the texture recalls apple pie, tricking our brains into thinking we're eating an actual apple pie. Mock apple pie dates to the mid-1800s: during the wintertime, when apples were scarce, home cooks substituted soda crackers or stale bread.

Then along came Ritz Crackers. When Nabisco introduced the golden crackers in 1934, they wisely named them "Ritz," offering "a bite of the good life" to a country dealing with economic hardship. They were an instant hit: by 1935, Nabisco had sold five billion boxes of Ritz crackers. When the recipe for mock apple pie appeared on the back of the boxes soon after, the inexpensive pie became a Depression-era dessert standard.

Mashed Potato Fudge

CCC cook Fatts Marr made this often, much to the delight of the enrollees at Camp Sapona in Southport, North Carolina. Anita Pritchard includes a similar recipe in the 1978 edition of her *Candy Cookbook*, noting, "Uncooked

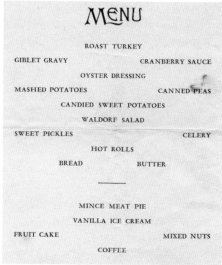

CCC Thanksgiving menu. *FDR Presidential Library & Museum.*

potato fondant is an old pioneer recipe so no one knows its source. I received this from an elderly lady in Kentucky, who wrote, 'It was given to me by my grandmother, who always served it in frilly cups or used it as a base for mint patties at Christmas time.'"

POOR MAN'S FRUITCAKE

Although desserts were a luxury during the Depression, creative cooks figured out substitutions for costly ingredients. Shortening replaced butter; water, milk. Baking powder was a popular substitute for eggs. This recipe is typical of the era, with no milk, butter or eggs, making it a budget-friendly holiday dessert with inexpensive, pantry-ready ingredients.

MINCEMEAT PIE

Invented as a means of preserving meat without salting or smoking, reminiscent of the heavily spiced meats of medieval times, mincemeat pies were born in England, where they remain a cherished holiday tradition. At first, meat was more plentiful than fruit in mincemeat pie, hence its name. This version replaces beef with suet (beef fat), so it retains its rich taste while also allowing the fruits to shine. Allow the pie to chill for three days before serving for an even richer flavor.

PRUNE PUDDING

Eleanor Roosevelt's values extended into the White House kitchens. She consulted with the home-economics faculty at Cornell, crafting menus that reflected the creative and budget-minded cookery employed by smart home cooks across the United States during the Great Depression.

"The mother of a family should look upon her housekeeping and the planning of meals as a scientific occupation," she wrote in her book *It's Up to the Women*.

Franklin and Eleanor Roosevelt seated on the south lawn at Hyde Park. Photograph by Oscar Jordan. August 1932. *FDR Presidential Library & Museum.*

Eleanor Roosevelt enjoys lunch at a Civilian Conservation Corps camp in Yosemite, California, 1941. *FDR Presidential Library & Museum.*

As I look back over the actual measures which were undertaken in this first year (of FDR's presidency), I realize that the one in which my husband took the greatest pleasure was the establishment on April 5, 1933, of the Civilian Conservation Corps camps.

—Eleanor Roosevelt

Roosevelt believed that it was possible to put a nutritious meal on the table even on a limited budget.

Whether or not the austere meals she served during her tenure at the White House were tasty is up to debate.

Ernest Hemingway noted after dining at the White House in 1937, "We had a rainwater soup followed by rubber squab, a nice wilted salad and a cake some admirer had sent in. An enthusiastic but unskilled admirer."

Senator Hiram Johnson wrote to his son after dining with the Roosevelts, "We had a very indifferent chowder first, then some mutton served in slices already cut and which had become almost cold, with peas that were none too palatable, a salad of little substance and worse dressing, lemon pie, and coffee."

In her efforts to maintain a humble, economical menu in the White House, Eleanor Roosevelt famously served prune pudding as dessert during the Depression. Prunes were not only inexpensive and widely available, but they also stayed fresh longer than other fruits used in puddings and pies. The recipe originally called for leaving the unpitted prunes in water overnight.

"She-She-She" Camps

The CCC was only open to young men. But did you know there were also "She-She-She" camps?

Eleanor Roosevelt loved the CCC ideal of employing young men in conservation and forestry. But what about the thousands of women in the United States who struggled with homelessness and unemployment?

"As a group, women have been neglected in comparison with others," the first lady said, "and throughout this depression have had the hardest time of all." Indeed, the number of women seeking jobs grew to two million by 1933.

She-She-She camp in Atlanta, Georgia. *FDR Presidential Library & Museum.*

She-She-She camp in Maine. *U.S. National Archives and Records Administration.*

She-She-She enrollees in Fera, New Jersey, 1934. Eleanor Roosevelt organized the nation-wide She-She-She Camps as a counterpart to the men-only focused CCC. Over 8,500 women served in She-She-She Camps. *U.S. National Archives and Records Administration.*

Feminist writer Meridel Le Sueur summarized the disastrous plight of unemployed women at the time: "[Jobless women] will go for weeks verging on starvation, crawling in some hole, going through the streets ashamed, sitting in libraries, parks, going for days without speaking to a living soul like some exiled beast."

At a time when many considered a woman's sole role as that of homemaker, Eleanor Roosevelt boldly came up with a plan to establish CCC camps that would serve women in need by teaching them valuable employment skills. She won the support of Labor Secretary Frances Perkins, and on June 10, 1933, the first all-female "She-She-She" camp, Camp TERA (Temporary Emergency Relief Assistance), later called Camp Jane Addams, situated on the rugged mountains rising from the west bank of the Hudson River, a site that would one day become Bear Mountain State Park, welcomed seventeen young women from New York City. By 1936, there were ninety women-only Civilian Conservation Corps camps, cleverly nicknamed She-She-She Camps.

It was about midnight on Christmas Eve in our CCC barracks when I heard the wind pick up and start blowing around our building. It was rattling the big doors at both entrances, shaking the windows over our bunks and tree branches brushed back and forth over the roof and walls. We could feel cold air coming up through the cracks in the floor, too.

We pulled our sheets and blankets closer around our shoulders. We had good spring beds with clean sheets and covers, so we were warm. Down the center aisle of the barracks were two wood-burning stoves that the night watchman refueled every hour as he passed through, checking everything in the camp.

It was my second Christmas in the CCC, but we didn't dwell on thoughts of home or of what they might be doing there. We were glad we had work to do and a place to eat and sleep. All of our wants were being taken care of by the government. I personally didn't think of my future; I realize now....

As I lay in my bunk thinking about Christmas dinner, the fire bell rang and rang. The whole camp was ordered out to fight a fire. Three or four trucks loaded up with about twenty-five men each and took off.

It seemed that "PeeWee," our lookout tower man, hadn't gone up to look around at his usual time that morning, thinking because of the snow, there was no danger of fires. Now, as he looked to the northwest, he saw a huge black hole in the timber, burning furiously. The winds had really whipped up some 400 acres into flames.

We sat on wooden boards that rested on the stakes of the truck and rode facing rear, away from the cold. There was a large box up behind the cab that carried all our tools.

As we got near the fire, we could see that it was mostly a leaf-ground fire and our fire-rakes could take care of it. But it still wasn't easy, for the wind was still strong, and you had to be careful. Besides that, the forest floor was stony and rough, with lots of 18" to 24" high wild huckleberry bushes....

We worked for hours and finally about dark we had the fire licked. As we rode back to camp, there wasn't much conversation except as to why "PeeWee" hadn't gone up to his place in the tower at the regular time. There was poor supervision somewhere.

As we pulled into camp, we saw Pop Emerson waving. He shouted, "Come on, boys, we saved your Christmas dinner till now!" Everything! We couldn't believe it. And it was good.

Later we found the cause of the fire. Some coon hunters had treed a raccoon in a large, dead, white oak and, being unable to get him down, set fire to the tree. He was either holed up or had moved to another tree. So they sat around drinking and celebrating. We found the whiskey bottles lying around the area. After a while, they got tired and cold and left. The tree was still burning and caught the woods on fire.

That was an unforgettable Christmas.

—Howard F. York, CCC enrollee from August 1934 to August 1936, Reform, Arkansas

In 1937, the National Youth Administration (NYA), a New Deal agency designed to provide work and education for young men and women between the ages of sixteen and twenty-five, decided that the women's program was too costly and shut down the She-She-She camps.

Over 8,500 women benefited from the She-She-She camps before they were closed.

Tomato Soup Spice Cake
with Cream Cheese Frosting

A spice cake featuring a can of condensed tomato soup? This classic and unique single-layer cake spiked with raisins and nuts calls for a secret ingredient: a can of condensed tomato soup. According to the Campbell's

When Chapter 556 of the Civilian Conservation Corps arrived at Pokagon in 1935, they planted trees and carved out nine scenic trails that are still in use today. During the spring and summer months, the men were busy building the park's stone and log structures, including the Gate House and Saddle Barn. When the winter months left the crew of eighteen- to twenty-three-year-olds snowbound, they set out to realize a toboggan track atop a hill just outside their camp for the sheer joy of it. Chapter 556 couldn't keep the fun to themselves, and in 1938, the park manager decided to open the toboggan hill to the public. The beloved attraction is still enjoyed by park visitors today. *Author photo.*

Soup company website, the recipe for tomato soup spice cake first appeared in an undated cookbook from approximately the late 1920s or early 1930s. In 1949, the cake recipe appeared in the *New York Times*, and in 1960, it became the first recipe to appear on a soup label.

SUGAR CREAM PIE

Sugar cream pie boasts a smooth filling of flour, butter, salt, vanilla, cream and brown sugar. It's also known as desperation pie because since it requires no fruit, you can easily make it year-round, with basic ingredients most home cooks already have on hand. As the unofficial state pie of Indiana, it was served at CCC camps across the Hoosier State.

BLACK BOTTOM PIE

Black bottom pie is typically served in the dead of winter when lemons are widely available. The recipe likely originated in the South, where many claim that it represents the Mississippi River, with its bottom layer of cocoa cream. Popular in the 1930s, the easy icebox pie was likely named after the 1925 hit jazz tune "Black Bottom Stomp," composed by pianist Jelly Roll Morton and inspired by the eponymous Detroit neighborhood.

The following recipe is adapted from one featured in the November 22, 1931 edition of the *Brownsville (TX) Herald*.

HERSHEY'S MOCHA DEVIL'S FOOD CAKE

The beloved U.S. chocolate brand Hershey's began in Philadelphia, where eighteen-year-old Milton Snavely Hershey opened his first candy shop in 1876. Hershey would experience several setbacks before finding success: credit issues led to the closure of his candy shop. In 1886, he launched Lancaster Caramel Company in 1886, only to switch to chocolate after seeing chocolate-manufacturing machines for the first time at the 1893 World's Columbian Exposition in Chicago. "Caramels are just a fad, but chocolate is a permanent thing," he predicted. By 1899, he had developed the innovative Hershey process, which is less sensitive to milk quality and uses a lesser amount of cocoa beans, thus minimizing costs.

In 1934, the *Hershey's Cookbook* was published, bringing the brand into home kitchens and mess halls across the United States.

JELL-O ICE CREAM

In 1897, carpenter and cough syrup maker Pearle Bixby Wait of Le Roy, New York, trademarked a gelatin dessert called "Jell-O" after experimenting with his wife at home, adding flavoring to granulated gelatin and sugar. Made with two ingredients that can easily be stored, it was a popular replacement for real, fruit-based ice creams in the 1930s.

You can use any flavor of Jell-O to make this no-churn ice cream—strawberry, cherry, lime, lemon, raspberry.

The CCC had a great impact on Glacier National Park. Thousands of men worked on projects inside of Glacier over the course of seven years. *Dave Sizer, Flickr.*

CCC crews stationed at Glacier National Park in Montana were said to be the "mainstay of the park labor organization" in the 1930s. CCC crews installed telephone lines over Logan Pass; prepared 150 acres of campground sites; and built trails, roads, and water and sewer systems. "These and thousands of other jobs were accomplished by these boys in the years they were in the park—many of them jobs that could not have been accomplished otherwise because of the high costs involved," notes the park's website. *NPS / Glacier National Park.*

Mock Apple Pie

For the Crust

2 cups all-purpose flour

1 teaspoon salt

1 cup shortening, cut into small pieces and frozen for 30 minutes

½ cup ice-cold water, or as needed

Optional: dust with ground nutmeg

Combine the flour and salt in a large bowl. Using a pastry blender, cut the shortening into the dry ingredients. Add the water and mix vigorously. Turn the dough out onto a lightly floured surface and knead until you can roll it out into a smooth ball. Put the dough on a sheet of plastic wrap and refrigerate for about one hour. With a rolling pin, flatten into a ⅛-inch-thick disk and place in a pie pan. Roll out a second disk, transfer to a baking sheet, and chill for at least 15 minutes.

For the Mock Apple Filling

36 Ritz Crackers

2 cups water

2 cups sugar

2 teaspoons cream of tartar

2 tablespoons lemon juice

Zest of one lemon

3 tablespoons of butter

Cinnamon

Preheat the oven to 425 degrees. Break Ritz Crackers into small, coarse pieces.

In a saucepan, combine water, sugar and cream of tartar and gently boil for 15 minutes.

Add the lemon juice and zest and let the mixture cool for a bit. Place the mixture in a pie tin lined with bottom crust.

Then pour the syrup over the crackers, dot with the butter and sprinkle with cinnamon.

Cover with the top crust, flute edges, and cut slits in the top crust to let steam.

It isn't enough to talk about peace. One must believe in it. And it isn't enough to believe in it. One must work at it.

—Eleanor Roosevelt

Bake the pie for 15 minutes and then place tinfoil around the edge to prevent over-browning. Bake for about 15 minutes longer or until the crust is golden brown.

Mashed Potato Fudge

½ cup unseasoned, well-mashed cooked potato (about 1 medium potato)
3 cups confectioners' sugar
1 cup flaked coconut
1 teaspoon vanilla extract
2 squares semisweet chocolate

While the potato is hot, beat in sugar and coconut, then vanilla.
Press into a lightly greased 8-inch square pan.
Melt chocolate and pour over top.
Chill and cut into squares.
Store in an airtight container in the refrigerator.

Variations

Vanilla Coconut Mashed Potato Fudge Balls. Omit chocolate from the recipe above. Combine mashed potatoes, sugar, coconut and vanilla in a mixing bowl and cream. Chill for several hours. Remove and turn onto a greased surface. Knead with hands until mixture is creamy and shape into one-inch balls. Place in candy papers and serve. Store in an airtight container.

Tennessee Christmas Mints. Omit vanilla and substitute a few drops of peppermint oil. Tint fondant pink with food coloring. Flatten balls to about ½-inch thickness.

Candied Fruit Balls. Omit vanilla and substitute rum, lemon or maple flavoring. Add ½ cup finely chopped candied fruit, such as cherries, pineapple, apricots or dates. Dried orange or lemon peel can also be used. Allow confections to dry at room temperature for at least 24 hours. These keep well at room temperature for two weeks if covered with plastic wrap.

Rice Krispie Macaroons

2 egg whites
1 cup brown sugar
2 cups Kellogg's Rice Krispies
½ cup chopped nuts (almonds, pecans or walnuts)
1 cup coconut
½ teaspoon vanilla extract

Beat egg whites until they are stiff enough to hold their shape, but not until they lose their shiny appearance. Fold in brown sugar carefully. Fold in Rice Krispies, chopped nuts and coconut. Add vanilla. Drop on a well-greased baking sheet.

Bake at 350 degrees for 15 to 20 minutes. Remove pans from the oven, place on a damp towel and remove macaroons immediately with a spatula or sharp knife. If macaroons become hardened, place back in the oven for a few minutes to soften.

Poor Man's Fruitcake

1 cup vegetable shortening

2 cups water

2 cups raisins, dates, apricots or any chopped, dried fruit

1 teaspoon ground cinnamon

1 teaspoon ground nutmeg

1 teaspoon ground allspice

1½ cups brown sugar

3 cups all-purpose flour

1 teaspoon baking soda

Optional: Confectioners' sugar

Preheat the oven to 350 F degrees. Grease and flour a 9x13-inch cake pan.

In a saucepan over medium heat, combine shortening, water, dried fruit, cinnamon, nutmeg, allspice and brown sugar and stir until the mixture reaches a boil.

Reduce heat to low and simmer for 10 minutes. Remove from heat and cool to room temperature.

Stir the flour and baking soda into the cooled dried fruit mixture.

Pour the batter into the prepared cake pan.

Bake for 30 minutes or until a toothpick comes out clean.

Serve cooled with a dusting of confectioners' sugar.

Wacky Cake

Wacky Cake is so rich and chocolatey that you won't even realize it contains no eggs, milk or butter, precious 1930s ingredients.

3 cups flour

2 cups sugar

1 teaspoon salt

2 teaspoons baking soda

⅓ cup unsweetened baking cocoa

2 cups water

3 tablespoons vegetable oil

2 tablespoons white vinegar

1 teaspoon vanilla extract

Preheat the oven to 350 degrees. Grease a 9x13-inch baking dish and set aside.

Mix flour, sugar, salt, baking soda and unsweetened baking cocoa in a large bowl. Set aside.

In a medium bowl, whisk together wet ingredients.

Stir wet ingredients into dry ingredients until thoroughly combined.

Pour batter into greased baking dish.

Bake for 30 minutes, or until a toothpick inserted into the center comes out clean. Allow to cool completely before frosting.

Fudge Frosting

1½ cups sugar

3 tablespoons unsweetened baking cocoa

⅓ cup milk

⅓ cup butter

1 teaspoon vanilla extract

In a medium saucepan over medium heat, whisk sugar, unsweetened baking cocoa, milk and butter until the mixture reaches a rolling boil. Stir for three more minutes until thickened.

Remove from heat and allow to cool for ten minutes. Whisk in vanilla extract. Pour warm frosting over the top of the cooled cake and smooth with a spatula. The frosting will harden as it cools.

Lemon Cake

Like other Depression-era cakes, this recipe doesn't call for eggs, butter or milk.

1½ cups flour
1 cup sugar
1 teaspoon baking soda
1 teaspoon salt
1 teaspoon white vinegar
4 tablespoons vegetable oil
1 cup water
1 teaspoon pure vanilla extract
1 teaspoon pure lemon extract (or the juice and zest of two fresh lemons)

Preheat the oven to 350 degrees.

Mix the flour, white sugar, baking soda and salt.

Whisk in the vinegar, vegetable oil, water, vanilla and lemon extracts and pour into a greased 8-inch square baking pan.

Bake on the middle rack of the oven for 30 minutes or until a toothpick comes out clean. Give the cake about a half hour to cool, then glaze.

Lemon Glaze

1 cup powdered sugar
1 tablespoon lemon juice, freshly squeezed
2 teaspoons freshly grated lemon zest
1 tablespoon milk

Whisk the ingredients until smooth. Drizzle over the lemon cake.

Apricot Upside-Down Cake

2 (15-ounce) cans apricot halves

¼ cup butter, cubed

½ cup light brown sugar

⅔ cup flour

1 teaspoon baking powder

¼ teaspoon salt

2 large eggs, separated

⅔ cup sugar

Preheat the oven to 350 degrees. Drain the apricots but reserve three tablespoons of the syrup and set aside.

Grease a 9-inch square baking dish with butter. Sprinkle evenly with the brown sugar. Arrange the apricot halves in a single layer over brown sugar, cut side up.

In a mixing bowl, whisk flour, baking powder and salt.

In a separate mixing bowl, whisk egg yolks until slightly thickened. Whisk in the reserved apricot syrup. Gradually add sugar, and whisk until well blended. Fold in flour mixture.

In a separate mixing bowl, whisk egg whites until stiff peaks form. Fold into batter. Spoon over apricots.

Bake for 40 minutes, or until a toothpick inserted in the center comes out clean. Cool for at least 10 minutes, then invert onto a plate to serve.

Mincemeat Pie

For the Pie Crust

2 cups all-purpose flour

1 teaspoon salt

1 cup shortening, cut into small pieces, and frozen for 30 minutes

½ cup ice-cold water, or as needed

For the Mincemeat

3 apples, peeled and chopped
1 cup dried figs, apricots or prunes, chopped
1 cup raisins
1 cup currants
¾ cup brown sugar
3 ounces finely chopped cold beef suet
⅓ cup brandy
2 teaspoons lemon zest
2 teaspoons orange zest
1 teaspoon allspice
1 teaspoon cinnamon
1 teaspoon ginger
1 teaspoon salt
1 large egg, mixed with one tablespoon of water
Sugar
Optional: whipped cream

Combine the flour and salt in a large bowl. Using a pastry blender, cut the shortening into the dry ingredients. Add the water and mix vigorously. Turn the dough out onto a lightly floured surface and knead until you can roll it out into a smooth ball. Put the dough on a sheet of plastic wrap and refrigerate for about 1 hour. With a rolling pin, flatten into a ⅛-inch thick disk and place in a pie pan. Roll out a second disk, transfer to a baking sheet and chill for at least 15 minutes.

Make the filling by mixing all the filling ingredients, making sure that the suet is evenly distributed. Chill the filling for about one hour.

Spoon the mincemeat into the pie dough-lined pan. Place the second pie crust on top of the mincemeat-filled pie, trimming and then crimping the crust edges. Brush with egg mixture and sprinkle with sugar.

Bake pie for 50 minutes to 1 hour or until golden brown. Let cool to warm or room temperature before slicing. Serve with whipped cream.

Prune Pudding

½ pound (about 2 dozen) pitted prunes
½ cup sugar
1 teaspoon cinnamon
1 cinnamon stick
3 tablespoons cornstarch

Place prunes in a medium-size saucepan with 2 cups of hot water and let soak for 1 hour.

In a saucepan, bring the soaked prunes to a boil. Reduce heat to low and simmer, covered, for about 10 minutes.

Drain prunes, saving the water, and chop. Add more hot water to the reserved prune water for a total of 2 cups. Place prunes and prune water back in the saucepan and add the sugar, cinnamon and cinnamon stick. Stir to combine and bring to a boil. Reduce heat to low and simmer for 10 minutes.

In a separate bowl, whisk the cornstarch and 2 tablespoons of cold water. Pour into the prune mixture and cook over low heat for about 5 minutes, stirring constantly, until the mixture thickens. Remove the cinnamon stick and pour the pudding into ramekins. Chill in the refrigerator for about one hour before serving.

Do not stop thinking of life as an adventure. You have no security unless you can live bravely, excitingly, imaginatively; unless you can choose a challenge instead of competence.

—Eleanor Roosevelt

Corn Flake Brown Betty

7½ cups corn flakes

10 cups chopped apples

1½ cups brown sugar

1 tablespoon cinnamon

6 tablespoons butter

Put a layer of corn flakes in a buttered baking dish, then a layer of apples. Sprinkle with some sugar and cinnamon and dot with pieces of butter. Fill the dish with alternate layers of apples and corn flakes. Add a sprinkle of water to moisten.

Bake in a 380-degree oven until the apples are soft. Serve with whipped cream.

Tomato Soup Spice Cake with Cream Cheese Frosting

½ cup butter, softened

1 cup sugar

1 egg

1 teaspoon baking soda

1 teaspoon vanilla extract

1 can condensed tomato soup

1¾ cups flour

1 teaspoon ground ginger

1 teaspoon nutmeg

1 teaspoon cinnamon

½ teaspoon salt

1 cup raisins

1 cup chopped nuts

Preheat the oven to 350 degrees, and grease and flour a 9x13-inch cake pan.

In a large mixing bowl, cream together butter and sugar until smooth. Add the egg and mix for about 30 seconds.

Dissolve the baking soda and vanilla into the tomato soup and slowly add to the butter mixture.

Sift together the flour, ginger, nutmeg, cinnamon and salt in a separate bowl. Add to the butter mixture and mix until well combined. Stir in the raisins and nuts.

Bake for 30 minutes or until a toothpick comes out clean. When cool, frost with cream cheese frosting.

Cream Cheese Frosting

½ cup butter, softened
8 ounces cream cheese
4 cups confectioners' sugar
2 teaspoons vanilla extract

Beat softened butter and cream cheese until well blended. Add confectioners' sugar and vanilla and beat until creamy.

Cherry Roly Poly

1 tablespoon cornstarch
1 cup sugar
2⅓ cups sour red cherries
½ cup Kellogg's All-Bran
¾ cup milk
1½ cups flour
4 teaspoons baking powder
1 teaspoon salt
2 tablespoons sugar
¼ cup butter

Mix the cornstarch and sugar, add cherries and bring to a boil. Strain cherries from the juice.

Soak All-Bran in milk. Sift flour with baking powder, salt and sugar. Cut in shortening until mixture is like cornmeal.

Add All-Bran and milk, stirring only until flour disappears.

Turn onto a floured board. Knead lightly and roll into a ¼-inch thick sheet. Cut into a square with a floured knife; place a few of the cherries in the center of each square; moisten the edges, and fold to make a triangle, pressing edges firmly. Dot with butter and sprinkle lightly with sugar.

Bake at 425 degrees for about 15 minutes. Serve hot, covered with the juice and the remaining cherries reheated.

Refrigerator Ginger Snaps

16 tablespoons butter

1 cup sugar

1 cup molasses

½ cup Kellogg's All-Bran

3½ cups of flour

1 tablespoon ginger

1 tablespoon cinnamon

1 tablespoon baking soda

¼ teaspoon salt

Cream butter and sugar. Add molasses and All-Bran. Beat thoroughly. Sift dry ingredients and combine with creamed mixture. Shape into rolls about 1½ inches in diameter. Wrap in waxed paper and refrigerate until firm.

Slice very thin and bake on an ungreased cookie sheet for 10 minutes at 375 degrees.

Sugar Cream Pie

For the Pie Crust

2 cups all-purpose flour

1 teaspoon salt

1 cup shortening, cut into small pieces, and frozen for 30 minutes

½ cup ice-cold water, or as needed

Optional: dust with ground nutmeg

Combine the flour and salt in a large bowl. Using a pastry blender, cut the shortening into the dry ingredients. Add the water and mix vigorously. Turn the dough out onto a lightly floured surface and knead until you can roll it out into a smooth ball. Put the dough on a sheet of plastic wrap and refrigerate for about one hour. With a rolling pin, flatten into a ⅛-inch thick disk and place in a pie pan. Roll out a second disk, transfer to a baking sheet and chill for at least 15 minutes.

For the Filling

2 cups heavy whipping cream

1 cup sugar

½ cup flour

½ teaspoon vanilla extract

2 tablespoons unsalted butter, cut into ½-inch pieces

⅛ teaspoon freshly grated nutmeg

Preheat the oven to 400. Whisk the heavy whipping cream, sugar, flour and vanilla. Pour into the chilled crust, dot with the butter and sprinkle the nutmeg on top. Bake for 10 minutes.

Reduce the oven temperature to 350 and continue baking until the crust is golden and the filling is bubbly in spots, about 50 more minutes. Cover the crust edges with foil if they're browning too quickly.

Serve with a dash of nutmeg.

Black Bottom Pie

Graham Cracker Crust

½ cup sugar

1½ cups graham cracker crumbs

½ cup melted butter

Mix sugar and cracker crumbs. Then pour melted butter over. Place in a pastry pan and pat in shape. Bake in a 425-degree oven until brown, about ten minutes.

Bottom Cocoa Layer

1¾ cups milk

¾ cup sugar

4 tablespoons cocoa

4 tablespoons flour

3 egg yolks

1 teaspoon vanilla extract

Scald milk by cooking in a saucepan over medium heat, stirring until the milk is just about to boil (you'll see bubbles forming on the edges and steam rising).

Pour the scalded milk into a double boiler. Whisk in sugar, cocoa and flour and stir over medium heat until thick. Then add egg yolks and vanilla extract and cook 5 minutes longer, whisking constantly. Cool and pour into graham cracker crust.

Lemon Curd Layer

3 eggs

1 cup sugar

¾ cup freshly squeezed lemon juice

1 tablespoon gelatin

⅓ cup water

Beat egg yolks and half cup of the sugar. Add lemon juice. Pour the mixture into a double boiler and cook over low heat, stirring constantly, until thick. Remove from heat. Dissolve gelatin in the ⅓ cup water, and slowly pour the mixture into the egg yolks/sugar.

Beat the egg whites until stiff. Add the other ½ cup sugar and fold into the egg yolk mixture. Pour on the dark filling and set in the refrigerator until ready to serve.

Serve topped with whipped cream.

We didn't have much in the way of clothes, and all we had were army issued. If we had a date with a girl in town, we would borrow clothes from one another. For example, a young man might borrow pants from one guy and a shirt from another. On special occasions like Thanksgiving and Christmas, the camp would provide a big dinner in the main halls, and we were allowed to invite someone from out of town, such as a girlfriend. We looked forward to these events because they meant good food and good company, but sharing clothes became more difficult because everyone wanted to look good.

—Frank Davis, Civilian Conservation Corps Company 411

Hershey's Mocha Devil's Food Cake

4 squares Hershey's baking chocolate, melted

2 egg yolks

1 cup milk

½ cup butter

1¾ cups light brown sugar

2½ cups flour, sifted

1½ teaspoons baking soda

½ teaspoon salt

1 cup black coffee

2 teaspoons vanilla

Melt the baking chocolate over simmering water, then add the egg yolks, then the milk, whisking constantly. Cook until thick and smooth. Cool and set aside.

In a separate bowl, cream the butter and sugar together.

In yet another separate bowl, mix the flour, baking soda and salt. Whisk into the creamed mixture. Whip in the coffee and chocolate mixture and beat well. Finally, whisk in the vanilla.

Pour into a greased and floured cake pan, and bake at 325 degrees for about 30 minutes, or until a toothpick comes out clean. When cool, ice with Chocolate Butter Icing.

Chocolate Butter Icing

3 squares Hershey's baking chocolate

6 tablespoons butter

2 egg yolks

1 teaspoon vanilla

1 cup confectioner's sugar

Melt the baking chocolate in the top of a double boiler over simmering water. In a separate bowl, cream the butter, egg yolks and vanilla, and slowly add melted baking chocolate. Add sugar and whisk until the icing reaches a thick consistency for spreading.

Jell-O Ice Cream

Jell-O (small box, any flavor)
Vanilla ice cream

Follow the package directions, boiling your water and whisking water and gelatin until fully dissolved.

Add in two cups of vanilla ice cream and whisk until well combined.

Pour equally into individual serving dishes and transfer to the refrigerator until fully set, about 30 minutes to an hour. Keep refrigerated until ready to serve. Top with whipped cream or sprinkles for extra flair.

LARGE-BATCH DESSERTS

One Hundred Molasses Cookies

4½ cups shortening

6 cups sugar, plus 1 cup for rolling

1½ cups dark molasses

6 large eggs

7 cups flour

6 tablespoons ground ginger

3 tablespoons ground cinnamon

2½ tablespoons baking soda

1 tablespoon salt

Preheat the oven to 350 degrees. Line baking sheets with parchment paper.

In a large bowl, mix shortening and granulated sugar. Add molasses and eggs and mix until combined.

In a separate large bowl, combine flour, ginger, cinnamon, baking soda and salt. Add flour mixture to wet mixture and beat until combined.

Pinch off small amounts of cookie dough and roll into 1-inch balls. Roll each ball in granulated sugar and place 2 inches apart on the baking sheet.

Bake until cookies are slightly cracked, about 12 minutes. Let cookies sit on the baking sheet for 5 minutes, then transfer to a cooling rack. They will flatten and the tops will further crack more while cooling.

One Hundred Oatmeal Cookies

14½ cups sugar

2 pounds (8 sticks) butter

1 tablespoon cinnamon

2 cups milk (or a 12-ounce can evaporated milk)

6 eggs

12 cups flour

2 tablespoons baking powder

8 cups oats

2 cups raisins

Cream the sugar, butter and cinnamon. Add milk and eggs and mix well.

Sift the flour and baking powder in a separate bowl and mix in the oatmeal. Add to the creamed mixture. Mix in the raisins.

Roll out the dough about ¼-inch thick and cut into round cookies.

Place on a well-greased baking pan and bake at 350 degrees for 15 minutes, or until golden.

Most of you are no doubt glad you are going home. But do not forget what your enrollment in the CCC has done for you. It has developed your body, and set you out with the idea that you are a fully grown man. Helped you to help yourself. To look into the future with a new and brighter aspect.

—*Canyon Echo*, March 30, 1938

Sugar Cookies for One Hundred

6 cups flour

2 teaspoons salt

2 teaspoons baking soda

2 teaspoons baking powder

1 pound (4 sticks) butter

3 cups sugar

3 eggs

1 tablespoon vanilla

5 tablespoons milk

Mix flour, salt, soda and baking powder and set aside.

Cream butter and sugar. Add eggs, vanilla and milk. Slowly add in the flour mixture, one to two cups at a time, and mix well.

Cover the cookie dough with plastic wrap and refrigerate for at least two hours or overnight.

Preheat the oven to 350 degrees.

Scoop dough by teaspoonfuls, roll into balls and then place on a cookie sheet. Use a kitchen glass dipped in white sugar to flatten the balls of dough.

Bake for about 12 minutes or until golden. Let set on a cookie sheet for about 3 minutes, then transfer to the cooling rack.

⁓

Baked Apples for One Hundred

100 apples

2 pounds (4½ cups) sugar

3 tablespoons cloves, ground

3 tablespoons nutmeg, ground

Wash the apples and remove the cores, but do not peel. Sprinkle the apples while wet with the sugar and spices. Place in a pan and bake at 325 degrees for about 1 hour or until tender. Serve hot or cold.

CCC boys leaving camp for home, Lassen National Forest, California. *Gerald W. Williams Collection, Wikimedia Commons.*

Bread Pudding for One Hundred

4 pounds fruit, fresh, canned or dried

20 pounds bread crusts or dry bread

4 (12-ounce) cans evaporated milk, diluted with 4 cups water

4 pounds (9 cups) sugar

3 tablespoons cinnamon

12 eggs, beaten

4 pounds raisins (9 cups)

If fresh fruit is used, peel, trim, core, etc., and cook, but not until mushy. If canned fruit is used, no cooking is necessary. If dried fruit is used, soak 8 hours or overnight in cold water and cook until tender.

Soak the bread in milk; add the sugar, cinnamon, beaten eggs and raisins; and mix well. Spread a layer of this mixture about 1 inch deep; spread a layer of fruit about 1 inch deep, then another layer of the bread mixture.

Sprinkle sugar and cinnamon over the top layer. Bake for about 40 minutes in a 325-degree oven. Serve hot or cold with milk or sweet sauce.

Sweet Sauce

9 pounds (32 cups) sugar

1 cup cornstarch

1½ gallons of water

¼ pound (1 stick) butter

¼ cup vanilla extract

1 tablespoon salt

Mix sugar and cornstarch, stir into boiling water and boil until slightly thickened, stirring constantly. Add butter, vanilla extract and salt, and cook until thick. (The sauce will thicken more after it chills, so do not cook down too much.). This sauce can be made richer by using milk in place of all or a part of the water.

Variations of this sauce can also be made by adding pureed cooked fruit or maple extract.

Ocean Path, Acadia National Park, Maine. When the CCC arrived at Maine's Acadia National Park, "it was still rural, small, and undeveloped," notes the park's website. The crew constructed many of the park's most popular trails, including the Ocean Path, the Perpendicular Trail. "The work was hard but fulfilling, and through their efforts, the CCC opened, protected, and beautified Acadia National Park." *Michael Tsai, Flickr.*

BIBLIOGRAPHY

Adams, Carol, Ed. *Favorite Recipes of the National Association of CCC Alumni.* Pocahontas Chapter 124 National Association of Civilian Conservation Corps Alumni, 1992.

Amberson, John, and Janney, Carrie. "Oral History Interview with Bill Stangl," National Park Service, September 1998. www.nps.gov.

Apps, Jerry. *The Civilian Conservation Corps in Wisconsin.* Madison: Wisconsin Historical Society Press, 2019.

Baldridge, Kenneth. *The Civilian Conservation Corps in Utah.* Salt Lake City: University of Utah Press, 2019.

Campbell's. "A Spicy History of Campbell's Tomato Soup Spice Cake." www.campbellsoupcompany.com.

Chen, Yong. *Chop Suey, USA: The Story of Chinese Food in America.* New York: Columbia University Press, 2014.

Davis, Frank. *My CCC Days: Memories of the Civilian Conservation Corps.* Parkway Publishers, 2006.

Fire Camp Cookbook. Missoula, MT: United States Department of Agriculture Forest Service, 1928.

General Foods CookBook. General Foods Corporation, 1932.

Giles, Janann. "CCC Food." *Capper's Farmer*, June 12, 2012. www.cappersfarmer.com.

Glatz, Peter. "Christmas Eve Oyster Stew." *Illinois Times*, December 2020. www.illinoistimes.com.

Hershey's Cookbook. Hershey, PA: Hershey Food Corp, 1934.

Hill, Edwin. *In the Shadow of the Mountain*. Pullman: Washington State University Press, 1990.

Hoyt, Ray. *Your CCC: A Handbook for Enrollees*. Happy Days Publishing Company, 1933.

Koeler, Jeff. "In WWI Trenches, Instant Coffee Gave Troops a Much-Needed Boost." National Public Radio, April 2017. www.npr.org.

Lacy, Leslie Alexander. *The Soil Soldiers*. Radnor, PA: Chilton Book Company, 1976.

Menu and Recipe Suggestions for U.S. Civilian Conservation Corps. Battle Creek, MI: Kellogg's, 1933.

Merrill, Perry. *Roosevelt's Forest Army*. Montpelier, VT: P.H. Merrill, 1981.

National Museum of Forest Service History. *Camp Cooking*. Layton, UT: Gibbs Smith Publishing, 2004.

National Park Service, Fort Pulaski National Monument. "An Oral History Interview with Civilian Conservation Corps members John West and Forrest Fields." July 28, 2000. digitalcommons.georgiasouthern.edu/ccc-pulaski-oral-histories.

Oliver, Alfred, and Harold Dudley. *This New America: The Spirit of the CCC*. Longmans, Green and Co., 1937.

An Oral History Interview with Civilian Conservation Corps Members, Joseph Whalen, Joe Czarnecki, George Haas, Make Lakomie, Hazel Feil, Peter Feil, and Andy Daino, interviewed by Elaine Harmon and Tom Hoffman. Sandy Hook, NJ: Gateway NRA, National Park Service, 1981.

Prichard, Anita. *Anita Prichard's Complete Candy Cookbook.* New York: Random House Value Publishing,1981.

Roosevelt, Franklin D. *The Public Papers and Addresses of Franklin D. Roosevelt.* Vol. 13. New York: Random House, 1938–50.

Sandweiss, Naomi. "Before WWII Began, a Generation of Jewish Men Joined FDR's 'Tree Army': On Tu B'Shevat, Recalling How Planting Trees in the Civilian Conservation Corps Helped Immigrants' Children Become Americans." *Tablet*, February 2, 2015. www.tabletmag.com.

School for Bakers and Cooks of the Fourth Corps Area. *Thirty Day Menus and Tested Special Recipes for CCC Companies.* N.p.: 1940.

Stienberger, Mabel C., and Miriam Birdseye. *Community Canning Centers.* Washington, D.C.: U.S. Department of Agriculture, 1935. archive.org/details/CAT31038847.

Subsistence Menus and Recipes for Feeding 100 Men for One Month. Chicago: Quartermaster Corps Subsistence School, 1933.

USDA Forest Service Fire Camp Cookbook. N.p.: 1928.

U.S. Senate. "Senate Bean Soup." www.senate.gov.

York, Howard. *I Can't Forget.* Kansas City, MO: Ebert Desktop Publishing, 1991.

ABOUT THE AUTHOR

Amy Bizzarri has written four books focused on Chicago history, but her experiences don't stop there. She's a teacher, tour guide, and certified wine expert. When she's not exploring her beloved Chicago by bicycle, you'll find her hiking the trails of a state or national park. Oh, yes, she's a mermaid, too, having trained with the celebrated sirens at Florida's Weeki Wachee Springs. Follow Amy's latest adventures at instagram.com/amybizzarri.

Visit us at
www.historypress.com
....